DISCARDED BY PC LIBRARY

PEN
S0-BGG-329

YOUR WORDS

Public and Private, Second Edition

Anne Passel

DATE DUE

UNIVERSITY
PRESS OF
AMERICA

45767

LANHAM • NEW YORK • LONDON

Copyright © 1981 by

University Press of America,™ Inc.

4720 Boston Way
Lanham, MD 20706

3 Henrietta Street
London WC2E 8LU England

All rights reserved
Printed in the United States of America

Library of Congress Cataloging in Publication Data

Passel, Anne.
  Your words, public and private.

    1. English language–Rhetoric. 2. Communication. I.
Title.
PE1408.P26   1981   808'.042   81–40773
ISBN 0–8191–1867–2 (pbk.)   AACR2

PE 1408
.P26

To the many students who have been
critics, editors, victims, and conquerors
of the English language in general
and this course in particular

Acknowledgements

Permission to reprint is gratefully acknowledged from the
following:

CALIFORNIA STATE COLLEGE, BAKERSFIELD STUDENT WRITERS: Carol
Anderson, "Will"; Lucinda Ware Austin, "Emergence of New" from
Saturday Mornings; Verna Banks Romondino, "Bias and Truth"; Judy
Bidart, "Death Dies," "Once More Around," "Gray Brown Bird," and
"After"; Elaina J. Bond, "On Conrad"; Michael Carriker, "The
Dragon Story"; Catherine Crown, "I Heard No Crying"; Janeen Guest
Smith, "Destination" from The Learning Poets, "Nowhere," and
"Private Blue"; John Hacharian, "Identification"; Peter
Leigh-Pink, "Rain" from The Learning Poet; Dwane Johnson for his
story; Barbara Sutliff, "On the Beach"; and Sharon Shires,
"Letters";

PROFESSIONAL CONSULTANTS: Murray Arnold on media; Lois Chaney,
Ward Fulcher, Stan O'Hara, and Grace Grant on evaluating student
work; Carl Miller for "My Ball Team" from California State
College, Bakersfield summer Reading Center;

AUTHORS AND PUBLISHERS: Harper and Row Publishers, Chatto and
Windus Ltd., and Mrs. Laura Huxley for Aldous Huxley,
"Centenaries" from On the Margin; J. M. Dent and Sons and the
Trustees of the Joseph Conrad Estate for Joseph Conrad, "The Congo
Diary" from Last Essays; Charles Scribner's Sons for Maxwell
Perkins letter in Editor to Author: The Letters of Maxwell E.
Perkins; American Association of University Women for "Consumer
Take Note" from AAUW Journal, August, 1973;

PHOTOGRAPHERS AND ARTISTS: Howard B. Passel, for photos of seed
shop, child in grass, dock scene, Charleston cemetery, Paris cat;
California State College, Bakersfield for photos of farmers and
parade; Paul Passel for child's drawing.

My special thanks to the Carnegie Corporation of New York which,
through a grant to the California State University and College,
supported the initial development of modules for this course.

Introduction

To communicate, what is it? It is sharing your feelings with someone else: your ideas, your reactions, your doubts, or your beliefs. You may communicate with a touch, with a gesture, by sharing activities or words. But in every case, you are successful when the person you are sharing with knows how you feel and what you think, knows and responds.

When you are with another person, this interchange of ideas is a kind of mutual activity. Your listener reads your expression as you read the listener's. If you think you are not communicating, you repeat yourself, try alternate words, substitute expressions. You convey your message by body language, raising and lowering your voice, leaning in, backing away, slowing your speech, hurrying through parts of your presentation. Your listener's response controls your delivery.

You have various ways of speaking -- we all have. You speak, for instance, in a formal style when you want to. Your sentences are correct, your words are carefully selected, and everything agrees properly. But somehow, at other times, this level sounds pretentious. In fact, the words change their meanings according to who the audience is. One word has several meanings, and every reader makes his own choice.

Mostly we use a kind of middle-level language, not the familiar fragmented special idiom used among friends or between brothers and sisters. But the middle level (what some call standard English) is the kind of language most of us use most of the time. This language is not specialized. It is not educationese, it is not crossword puzzle solving, it is not the result of an obsolete word hunt through Webster's or the thesaurus. It is just a kind of language most people use and understand and believe. In this course, we will look into the special problems of communication which you are going to face, and are now facing, as a functioning member of a community. It has been assumed, in setting up this course, that you have already had the basic composition courses, so that an emphasis on the MODES of writing will be most helpful for you.

When you trust your ideas to written words, you have a more complicated problem than you have when you speak. Communication is what involves us all, and almost all of the time. Written communication is a large part of this whole. You write for someone else. The reading audience is a silent audience -- at least it usually is. You very seldom know how your reader is reacting to your ideas. But you can assume, from the beginning, that the ideas that stay with your reader are the ideas which come in the appropriate words.

Now, what is "appropriate"? The word itself suggests that you must identify your audience before you formulate the first sentence of a communication.

Module I

In this module, all students will begin with the consideration of audiences. You will consider the importance of determining who your audience is to be

4

and how each kind of audience puts demands on you, influencing your vocabulary, the structure of your work, your sentence patterns, and the limitations you set for your subject matter.

Don't forget: it is not necessary to try and reach everyone when you write. One audience at a time is enough. In fact, you are your most successful when you select your audience and then hit the mark.

There was a time when the reader was firmly tied to the writer. Even today, a good rainy day may draw readers to the written word. But it is harder and harder to balance what you have to say on the one hand with what you feel for the reader on the other and be a successful writer. Some readers are resistant by nature. Some are too comfortable doing something else to bother to read. But when you do succeed, you take your reader with you wherever you want him to go. Special skill has got to come into play. You will enchant your reader, be a spellbinder. And when you do, what a good experience it is! You have your tools, words, and you know what the challenge is. Persuade him, make him believe, exert your powers.

Once you have done the four exercises in this module and have had your first conference, you will be ready to move on. You will select from Modules II through IX, according to your interest, your own particular need, and according to the requirements of the course. Whatever your selection, you will attend each of the demonstrations and discussions as they are listed in the syllabus.

These meetings are designed to supplement and reinforce the material in the book. Even if you are not planning to select the module under discussion, you will find these meetings a help in your own studying and in your individual conferences.

Module II

Do you remember what was taught in Freshman English about note taking and outlining? If not, this might be a good module to do next. Even if you do remember, but have not been practicing these skills, you may find this a valuable module. You may even encounter some ideas that are totally new. Good habits in pre-writing are worth striving for.

Module III

Here you are given the chance to practice controlling your public voice. You will start by thinking out the importance of point of view. In this course, we are referring to it as bias -- that is, what kind of predisposition you have toward the subject. In telling about any event, the one in the Garden of Eden for example, there could be three different versions of the situation, depending on the narrator. We all have bias; we are SUPPOSED to. What we want to do is accommodate our thinking to our own natural attitude. If you have a strong preference for dogs or for cats, you had better acknowledge that before you begin to write and compensate for it when you tackle a paper on cats.

You are not required to change your opinion about life, but merely to be aware that you write from a bias, as everyone does. Everyone sees something different when he looks out on life. You offer one view; that is your point of view. And actually, that is what makes you special. You have a point of view which you can bring to your audience.

Now, sometime or other you are going to find yourself selected to handle the publicity for some group: church or school, scouts or Campfire Girls, Rotary or AAUW. In Module III you will have the opportunity to work out the basic principles involved in public relations, what to get before your audience and how to handle releases and presentations. We will explore news sheets and newspapers, radio and television, and will learn the specific requirements of each medium.

Module IV

This section deals with another area of communication which involves us all: letter writing. First, we tackle that vital letter of application for a job, with attention to form and substance. Then a series of exercises deals with professional and business letters, and a closer examination of levels of style in letters to friends and acquaintances.

Module V

The subtleties of some other areas of language are covered in the module "Words, Words, Words." If you want to concentrate on how to develop word power, here is an appropriate module. A section follows on using such basics as time and tense, handling personal pronouns, selecting between singulars and plurals, and sensing the importance of the active over the passive voice. You will contrast the styles of Aldous Huxley, Mary Shelley, and Mark Twain.

Modules VI, VII, VIII, and IX

These modules deal with you as a creative writer, expressing yourself in your private voice. Not all of you will find that story-writing or poetry-writing is what you do best. But, from observing the experiences of other students who have taken this course, we can safely say that many of you who have never done creative writing will find that you have talent in the area, and will discover that writing is an exciting experience. Part of the inner workings of man demands the release of creative energy. Here is your chance to see whether this creative release is the right one for you.

This is not the ad which promises you a whole new career including fame and fortune, but you will find that writing fiction and poetry is a challenge. It is satisfying for the inner being, and it is a possible achievement. Yet even the most enthusiastic writer needs training in the fundamentals of the craft. And that is what you will be doing: learning the best way to handle language to be effective.

These modules offer you a bonus, besides. Even if

you are not planning to teach, you may need to know how to react to creative writers sometime in the future. Your husband or wife, your child, your friend may come to you one day and ask you to respond to a story or a poem. "That's nice" won't always satisfy. Especially in a classroom, the creative writer needs special treatment. When you too have been a creative writer you will find criticism and help much easier to give.

Module X

When you have finished all but one of the modules you have decided on, you will be ready for Module X -- your final module. This is called "Evaluation as a Skill." As you approach the climax of this module you will evaluate the work of another student who has taken this course. And then -- in the end -- judge yourself, checking what you have accomplished against the criteria you have set up.

Remember, in communicating, we are doing one of two things: giving information or persuading. One depends on the detached intellect, one on a controlled use of emotions. One deals with fact, one with feeling. Sometimes a judicious use of both is called for. But first you must decide what you are trying to do. Balancing on the line will not work. Writing is not always easy. Sometimes being effective with words is as hard as anything you can think of doing. Sometimes it turns into a battle royal. But that is what the course is all about.

Look over the material for this course. You follow

the assignment in the modules you have elected to take.
When they are completed, turn them in to your
instructor, a few days before your scheduled
conference. There are four kinds of learning
encounters in this course.

1) Printed material, now in your hands, which will
   direct you through a series of exercises
   designed to help you learn for yourself by
   writing.

2) A series of scheduled class meetings for
   demonstration and discussion of areas which are
   best learned by this method. (We may do
   experiments in observing and writing, hear a
   public relations expert, talk, listen to
   professional and student poets explaining about
   poetry, join with a panel of teachers while
   they discuss grading and evaluation of
   students.) Each of these sessions will include
   the writing of an in-class theme.

3) Time spent by yourself, exercising your
   abilities and defining your own specific needs.

4) Individual conferences for close examination of
   your progress. (These conferences are designed
   to cover the work in the module you have just
   completed.)

Are there tests? No. Is there a final? Not in
the usual sense. You will have your last conference
when you have completed Module X. You and the

instructor will go over your work and see what progress you have made.   This conference will emphasize the areas you should concentrate on in the future.

In this course, you are really in charge of your own learning.   But whenever you need assistance, clarification, help, encouragement, make an appointment for advice.   Your instructor is not merely a lecturer and a test-grader.   In this class, student and faculty member work together, one-on-one.

Module I

Determining the Audience

Module I

Determining the Audience

You might get the idea, from watching people in libraries and bookstores, that audiences select books. But the truth is that the selection is made the other way around: writers choose audiences. This process of selection takes place long before the book appears in its final form. The same can be said of all communication, including yours. Before you write a word you must have clearly in mind what audience you are writing for, and that decision is the most important one that you will make. It will affect the shape of what you write, the words you use, and the response you elicit.

How do audiences differ? Obviously in age: **Nursery Rhymes for Grown-ups** would be a far cry from what Mother Goose had in mind. But audiences differ too in their backgrounds and understanding, their interests and persuasions. Your readers' bias will affect the way you will approach them to convince them, and their cultural level and life experience must also be taken into consideration. If you write a publicity notice for the feature section of a newspaper, that is a particular audience. If you apply for a job and write your prospective boss, that is a different one. If you write a song to put a child to sleep, that is still another. In every case you recognize your audience, convey your message in a way that is highly acceptable, and stimulate your readers or listeners to thought or action (depending on what you have in mind).

Once you agree to this short pre-writing analysis of audience, your job of communication is enormously simplified. You know your audience, you know your message -- now all you have to do is be convincing.

Words and phrases

What kind of vocabulary will you use? Idioms which appeal to a limited group? Will you slip into a specialized jargon? Actually you must still bear in mind that there are **three** entities involved in this (or any) communication: the writer, the message, and the reader. While you are going to accommodate your style to the subject matter and the audience, remember that you will always maintain your own identity. Do not try to become something that you are not. You must find an area of mutual understanding between you and your reader. Through this commonality, you will be most persuasive.

Level of diction

You must already be aware that without shifting your personality in the slightest you are capable of communicating on several different levels. These are what we are calling your modes of writing and speaking. At the bottom you have your most colloquial and least orderly diction. This is what you use when you are mad, most harried, most distraught. You yell at your kids or your kid brothers, you curse your car or the vacuum cleaner, you say for the twenty-fifth time what a cretin should have understood on the first time through. This is not the level of language that you will put into writing. Slightly above this level is slang or colloquial repartee among close friends. Fine for the in-group but not much for the big world.

Now altogether on the other, elevated end, you have your most formal level of diction. If you congratulate your boss on his silver anniversary, this is what you probably use (though it may not be the most effective level you could use). You use it too to address the judge, the college president, the minister, the Honorable Director as he grants you the Award of Merit. On this level, your language is all pre-considered. The subject and verb agree, because you thought it out in advance. The sentences all have verbs and the modifiers all hang close to what they are meant to modify. It is stilted prose, probably, and the best that can be said for it is that it demonstrates that you actually know what is correct.

Somewhere between this exalted elegance and the casual colloquial talk is what we like to call standard English. It is free-flowing and natural, it is fresh and alive. We can hope that in it too the grammar is respectable and dependably traditional -- for clarity's sake. It is on this level that people communicate most effectively. Any audience you try to reach will understand you most easily when you speak out in standard English.

Pattern of the whole

The larger units of composition are at your disposal to help you write effectively. Sentences in

their various patterns -- simple, complex, compound --
can be shaped to appeal to any kind of audience.
Whatever the age or taste of the readers, they will
appreciate a natural speech cadence, and the younger
they are the more rollicking rhythm they will enjoy.
Logical sequence from sentence to sentence and
paragraph to paragraph will assure you that your reader
is having an easy time of it. The sense of completion
brought about by a unified whole -- beginning, middle,
and end -- will support whatever argument you propose
to whatever audience you select.

Tone

The mysterious quality of tone is the least
identifiable and most controlling element in your
writing. It is primarily to do with your own attitude
toward your subject matter and your audience. You must
understand the first and feel empathy for the second.
Maybe the other way around, too. You will say what is
clear and true and believable about your subject. You
will respect your audience, not deliberately offending
or condescending, but acting in the reasonable belief
that when they have heard you out, your readers will of
course want to believe as you believe. Give your
audience credit for intelligence, taste, and emotions.
But remember that there is a limit to each person's
understanding -- and to be effective you must ask your
readers to stretch just a little beyond their limit.
But if it will work out with your position, tell them
something they like to hear as well.

Module I

Unit A

Identification of Audiences

Not only do we shape our writing to suit the intended audience, but the process works in reverse. By carefully studying any particular passage we can identify what audience the author was trying to reach. Take for example the following passage:

And Ruth said, "Intreat me not to leave thee, or to return from following after thee; for whither thou goest, I will go; and where thou lodgest, I will lodge; thy people shall be my people, and thy God my God: where thou diest, will I die, and there will I be buried: the Lord do so to me, and more also, if ought but death part thee and me."

How will you begin to decide on the original audience this passage was intended for? First, whether you have recognized it or not, you can see that it is a direct quotation from a character in a story, whose name is Ruth. Now, ask yourself what distinguishes this kind of writing from something ordinary today.

First, you sense a very strong cadence, an inner rhythm which is almost sing-song, caused by repetition and patterning. This signifies that the work was originally composed to be listened to, not read. Such marked cadence could indicate a work for children, who are listeners, but the subject matter leads you to

19

conclude that such is not the case. This is a work from the Old Testament which was intended to be heard, remembered, and passed on by word of mouth. Its purpose was to teach about admirable behavior and about loyalty. You might not recognize the source but you could easily conclude that the work was originally intended for recitation.

But that is not all you can conclude. What about diction? We know we are not reading ancient Hebrew, yet the language is not the language of twentieth-century America. Such forms as "goest, lodgest, diest" and "thee, thou, thy" are not the forms most of us use today. They are English words, but not in common usage. It is not valid, though, to say this is "special Bible language." When was the Bible translated into the language we recognize as "Bible language"? If you recall the full information about the version familiar to most of us, you will recall that it is referred to as The King James Version. James I's dates? 1566-1625. Now we are ready to say that the diction indicates that this version was written in the late 16th or early 17th century and therefore in the language of that day. Parents of the day did not say, "Go play like your brother"; they said "Goest thou and do likewise," or some such phrase.

A further consideration leads to a rather startling conclusion: contrary to being in obscure and esoteric form and language, this passage is a direct urging toward loyalty and is intended to reach its first audience in a form easy to remember (the cadence) and in the common language of the time (that is, the time of the translation which we are reading). Application to relevant learning: if you have a message you want remembered, couch it in a rhythmic form, and use the language most easily accepted by the listener. (It helps, of course, if you achieve the particular beauty of a passage such as this one from **The Book of Ruth** I:16-17.)

Here are some passages intended for seven very different audiences.

1.

Once upon a time, on an uninhabited island on the shores of the Red Sea, there lived a Parsee from whose hat the rays of the sun were reflected in more-than-oriental splendor. And the Parsee lived by the Red Sea with nothing but his hat and his knife and a cooking stove of the kind that you must particularly never touch.

.   .   .   .   .

But the Parsee came down from his palm tree wearing his hat, from which the rays of the sun were reflected in more-than-oriental splendor, packed up his cooking stove, and went away in the direction of Orotavo, Amygdala, the Upland Meadows of Anatarivo, and the Marshes of Sonaput.

2.

Washington Public Power Supply System is a young, growing, dynamic major pacific northwest company engaged in the engineering and construction of five nuclear power plants. Our construction project is considered one of the largest in the U.S.

We have a need for Senior Personnel Professionals to fill restructured Management and Non-management positions within our organization in such areas as: Labor Relations, Compensation, Employment Relations and Recruitment. You must have at least five years experience.

Our employees receive excellent salaries, comprehensive benefit packages as well as numerous opportunities for professional growth and development.

3.

In the Beethoven he was relaxed and reflective, some rough edges notwithstanding. In the Mozart he was surprisingly aggressive, despite the application of some exquisite, illuminating detail. The ethereal Adagio lacked the wonted serenity, and the cadenzas attributed to Sam Franko seemed a bit ornate for stylistic comfort.

Stylistic problems emerged in the Baroque efforts, too: a harpsichord continuo realization so reticent it might be regarded as negligible; expressive indulgences that suggested a Romantic anachronism; ornaments arbitrarily applied . . .

22

AS THE WORLD TURNS: During a sexual tryst, Maggie told Tom she'll defend John. Tom's the prosecuting attorney. John was booked after Lyla phoned the cops and stole his gun so that he can't get even with Dee. Joyce licked her chops when Grant fell for her "dying act" and proposed marriage. Andrea denied to Kim that Andrea and Steve had an affair, but Kim realized that Andrea's lying in order to win back Nick. Jeff and Barbara were suspicious that Margo is hot to trot with James. Ellen blamed David for encouraging Dee to sign the rape complaint. Lyla failed to dissuade Maggie from being John's lawyer.

5.

It is gratifying that the Supreme Court has so resoundingly outlawed the federal government's surveillance of domestic "subversives" by wiretapping without benefit of a warrant. This 8 to 0 decision is a welcome affirmation that we must still be guided by the Fourth Amendment strictures against invasion of citizens' privacy without a specific order of approval from a court.

We approvingly quote from the ruling: "History abundantly documents the tendency of government -- however benevolent and benign its motives -- to view with suspicion those who most fervently dispute its policies. The price of lawful public dissent must not be a dread of subjection to an unchecked surveillance power. Nor must the fear of unauthorized official eavesdropping deter vigorous citizen dissent and discussion of government action in private conversations."

6.

An 11-year-old, 85-pound liberated lady rode to victory in the Phoenix Soap Box Derby.

"Well, I'm proving that girls aren't so dumb." said Jane Walters as she climbed into her sleek orange coaster car for the championship race Sunday against Mike Brenton, 13.

She streaked over the finish line scant inches ahead of her final competitor, topping 107 boys and nine other girls during the 99-degree afternoon.

Jane beat her best friend, Valerie Gaxiola, 11, on the way to winning a $500 scholarship and trip to the national race in Akron, Ohio, August 13.

"All the boys are jealous." Jane said after the final race. "They didn't think a girl would win."

7.

Tuesday, 19th
    General direction E.N.E. -- Dist^{ce} 15 miles.
    Sun visible at 6:30. Very warm day.
    Inkissi River very rapid; is about 100 yards broad. Passage in canoes. Banks wooded very densely, and the valley of the river rather deep, but very narrow.

Today did not set the tent, but put up in Gov^t Shimbek. Zanzibari in charge -- very obliging. Met ripe pineapple for the first time. On the road to-day passed a skeleton tied up to a post. Also white man's grave -- no name -- heap of stones in the form of a cross. Health good now.

Unit A. Assignment

Read over the passages carefully until you feel that you can sense the kind of person each passage was composed for.

List these audiences and point out at least one clue which led you to this conclusion.

Now carefully examine one of the passages, and in a brief but explicit essay identify the audience and explain how you made this identification. What elements in the passage led you to this conclusion? Look carefully into the subtleties of the writing.

Module I

Unit B

Transposition

Your audience puts its demands on you. You respond
by writing what they can read and what they will be
persuaded by. But this ideal arrangement is not always
possible. Sometimes we must communicate a less
congenial message to a predetermined audience. Imagine
such a situation.

Unit B. Assignment

Select two passages from those given in Unit A.

Rewrite the first passage you have chosen
giving the same main facts to the audience of
the second passage you have chosen.

Reverse the process and write the facts of the
second passage you selected for the audience of
the first one you chose. Include a brief
statement explaining how your revision has
changed the passages.

(Example: To avoid spoiling the exercise for you,
let's take two passages not included here. Let's take
the one from Ruth and one from a nursery rhyme, for
example, "This is the house that Jack built." Now you
would write the plea, "Be loyal and don't go away,"
(the facts give in the passage from Ruth) in terms

26

which would work for a child (the audience for the
nursery rhyme). You would then rewrite the condition
in that house which Jack built as though it were a
serious lesson from the Bible.)

Module I

Unit C

Appropriateness of Style

From any book you like, select a short typical passage. Write out the passage. Now analyze the material in relation to the intended audience. Look at all levels of the work: words, idioms, sentence pattern, overall structure, unity, tone, effectiveness of persuasion.

Unit C. Assignment

Write a comprehensive evaluation of the passage in relation to the intended audience. Answer these questions:

Do you think the author gauges the audience's level?

What are the most effective devices used?

Does the author miss the audience in any way?

Do not concern yourself with the author's choice of subject matter. Concentrate on **how** the material was used (vocabulary, sentence form, level of diction, syntax and cadence, structure of the whole).

Module I

Unit D

Appropriateness of Subject Matter

Yes, audience determines style, but subject matter may in turn determine audience. If cornered, we can tailor any subject to any given audience--well, **almost** any subject to **almost** any audience. But when we are not cornered it is another matter. Ordinarily we behave predictably. The process is: subject reaches writer; writer responds with idea; writer imagines proper audience for this idea; writer uses style appropriate for imagined audience.

Unit D. Assignment

Look at the pictures on the following pages. Select one which appeals to you. Now respond to the picture in any way you like.

Write your response as it would be presented to a particular audience, any audience you choose.

Include, at the end, an explanation of what audience you chose and what effective devices you used to reach that particular audience.

Module II

Being Organized

Module II

Being Organized

Into a professor's office comes a student. Let's say this one is male. He is a bright student, full of interesting ideas, odd scraps of quotations and information, a ready wit, wonderfully innovative approaches to old solidified theories, and a binder full of notebook paper. As he drops into the chair, he liberates a confetti flurry of small pieces of paper, ready to escape ever since yesterday when he ripped the sheets from his spiral notebook. Oozing from his binder are the curling edges of loose papers.

He makes an appointment for tomorrow: sprawling penciled numbers find a corner in the marked-up page. He keeps his good humor and air of having brought a moment's brightness into the drab professorial world.

Likeable? Very! Yet what kind of paper will he produce to be evaluated along with the growing stack of neatly typed, even-edged, clean covered, clearly presented, and rationally argued themes? If he is lucky (and he runs on luck) the professor will be so pleased with his ideas that he will not be distracted by fringed tear outs, dog paw-prints, and coffee stains. But why should anyone take that chance?

Neatness requires self-discipline; wanting to be orderly is the natural outcome of self-respect. For a period of time, anyway, your paper **is you**. Let it give you the best possible representation.

Module II

Unit A

Notecards

By the time we have become adults we have all worked out systems of organization that seem to work for us. The problem is, most of us, satisfied or not, hesitate to try new systems; preferring to "bear those ills we have than fly to others that we know not of."

But why not try something new? Look at your current approach to note-taking and paper-writing. Is it orderly? Flexible? Practical? Does it allow for change while, at the same time, offering you a clear visible control over your work in progress? The note-card system does.

Here are a few of the advantages:

Size	You have a choice of three easily-acquired cards
3 x 5	(if you are neat and have a small handwriting)
5 x 8	(too big to carry in your pocket -- also these may tempt you to put more than one idea per card)
4 x 6	(like the third bear's porridge -- just right. Compact, portable, modest, and a good size to be filed in a shoe box)
Color	Like adding another dimension for the categorizing and classifying of information

What goes on a card? Just one note or quotation. All card users have their own systems. This one uses a three-part coding: quoted material, paraphrase, and researcher's own ideas.

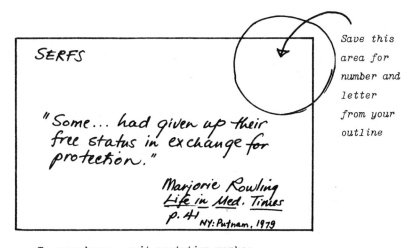

SERFS

"Some... had given up their free status in exchange for protection."

Marjorie Rowling
Life in Med. Times
p. 44 NY: Putnam, 1979

Save this area for number and letter from your outline

To paraphrase, omit quotation marks:
Some serfs wanted to be protected—
For your idea, based on the quotation, use square brackets:
[protection can be more imp. than self-assertion]

The advantages of cards in notetaking are numerous. When you read something pertinent, hear a good idea, have a brilliant thought, you reach into your pocket or purse, pull out a waiting card, and jot it down. When you get back to your desk you file the card and replenish your pack of blank cards.

As soon as you have gathered as many notes as you plan to gather, lay out your cards and look them over. You can now play a kind of academic solitaire, matching kinds and separating ideas. These piles can be arranged and rearranged. When you have found the

workable arrangement, fill in the box in the upper
right corner according to the outline which is taking
form as you work with the cards.

When you have finished the paper, file the cards
according to subject matter (not just as notes for this
paper). Many of them will be useful to you later, for
some other study.

Unit A. Assignment

Select three books with information in the same
general area. (If you are researching a paper for
another class, fine; use that material.)

Prepare a card (or outline a card on your paper) on
which you record a direct quotation. Be sure to copy
accurately -- including all punctuation -- and to give
the full documentation for the work (author, book
title, city of publication, publishing company, year of
publication, page or pages on which the quotation
appears).

Now, on another card, give the same material
paraphrased (you will need the same publication data).

Now, on another card, record an idea of your own
which came into being because of something an author
suggested (include same data).

If you like, add other kinds of notes you might
make on other cards.

Module II

Unit B

Outlining

Some people in college (and especially many in graduate school) never hand in a piece of writing that has not been outlined. Inside the cover of every bluebook you could find a small, private, and very essential outline. These people are not going to be caught having said everything they know on the first page and now stuck with a blank bluebook and the rest of the test period to fill with repetitions. Their outlined answers are the ones instructors can read easily and respond to positively.

Naturally, the most readable course papers are ones which have been outlined before they are written. Using the classifications determined by the physical arranging of notecards, the organized student now concocts an outline which gives balance and proportioned argument to the pending paper.

Let's consider the easiest and most basic outline known to writers. Everything arranges itself by threes. (Two works for comparison and contrast; four or more may often become unwieldy. Three is ideal.)

The first main division is: Introduction, Body, Conclusion. Within the body, let the material divide itself into three areas· I, II, III -- each one of the three main points you are going to make. Each of these might be supported by three strong reasons for believing that point (A, B, C). Each of these could be verified by proofs or quotations, examples or details (1, 2, 3).

Here is a hasty but orderly three-part outline:

Introduction: Thesis statement: To some, cats are not as appealing as dogs, but cats have always had a certain charm for many people.

Body: the qualities which cats have.

I. They are individualistic
   A. Independent
      1. "He walked by himself, and all places were alike to him" (Kipling)
      2. The Cheshire Cat "vanished quite slowly" (Lewis Carroll)
      3. The cat wanted fish "ac he nele his feth wete" (Ms. circa 1250)
   B. Aloof
      1. They walk "on little cat feet" (Sandburg)
      2. ". . . had Tiberius been a cat" (M. Arnold)
      3. ". . . vice in a cat" (Gail Hamilton)
   C. Condescending
      1. "A cat may look on a king" (Heywood)
      2. "A cat languishes loudly" (Henley)
      3. "I . . . make her more sport" (Montaigne)

II. They are instinctual
    A. ⎫
    B. ⎬ and so forth (you would fill this in, as
    C. ⎭ above)
III. They are traditional bearers of good fortune
    A. ⎫
    B. ⎬ and so forth (you would fill this in, as
    C. ⎭ above)

Conclusion: Some famous people have owned cats. I have a dog.

Unit B. Assignment

Prepare a skeletal outline (one without specific quotations or proofs) on **one** of the following subjects:

> My first attempt in self-improvement
> This week's most startling news
> How to -- (change a tire, cook an egg, return a ball, etc.)
> Equality in --

Use Introduction, Body, Conclusion. In the Body, use three main points; under each, three divisions; under each of those, three specific aspects, proofs, examples, etc.

Module II

Unit C

Determining Emphasis

After you have collected your resource material, sorted it (rejecting those notes which will not add anything to your paper), and organized it into an outline form, you are ready to write. Certain predetermined aspects of the paper will get you off to a good start:

Audience. What readers you are writing for?

Purpose. Why are you writing this presentation? What do you expect your reader to do when he has finished reading the paper?

Emphasis. What is your most convincing point? How do you intend to emphasize this point?

You have already looked into the influences which your audience has on your language, diction, syntax, patterning, and unity. Now identify the purpose of the work: is it a report of an existing condition, a proposal for improvement, a statistical account of the state of affairs, a recommendation or clarifiation of position? Then you must recognize what action (or reaction) you expect from your readers. All these considerations will help you determine the balance and emphasis of your paper.

Unit C. Assignment

Look over the outline you prepared for Unit B.

Explain briefly and clearly how you will use emphasis to make your essay convincing. Identify what would be your most effective approach if you were to write this theme.

Open: Do you make sure your readers know what you are writing about?

Sequence: Do you start with the most important idea and then become less forceful? Or do you end with your strongest point, building up to it?

Balance: Do you try to maintain equal reader-interest throughout? Or do you stress one high point or many?

Preparation: Are your readers taken by surprise? Or do you intentionally prepare them for your main idea?

Conclusion: Does your ending state a final unequivocal solution? Or do you leave an open end, giving your readers the chance to decide for themselves?

Module II

Unit D

Patterns of Presentation

Certain truths can be faced about reports. Many are dull; many are ineffectual; some seem to be informative, alive, important, and worth doing something about. What makes the difference?

First, put some organization onto the process of preparing the report: Think out what you hope to accomplish. Work out each part before you start on the whole. Keep in mind: clarity, purpose, emphasis.

Have this awareness in the front of your mind as you begin planning the report.

As for language, you **do not need** jargon. You do not need familiar phraseology and hackneyed expressions. You do not want slang or colloquialisms. You are a human being writing for another human being.

Create a viable pattern for your presentation, identifying the purpose of the report, the supporting facts, and your proposed conclusion. Try to deal with the questions we expect to have answered: who, why, what, where, when, and how; then propose a conclusion. Sometimes the pattern is based on progression, explaining a procedure followed.

Follow these steps in writing (and, of course, this

44

is after the research and organized activities have been successfully completed):

> Write your paper in the rough
> Read (aloud is most helpful)
> Type in its approximate form
> Proofread for content and form
> Type final form
> Final proof reading
> Check: is it clean, neat, and readable?

Unit D. Assignment

Take a paper you have previously written for this class or some other class and identify your pattern of presentation. Do not base your answers on your own private information; use proofs found in the paper.

Indicate the following:

> For whom was the paper written? How do you show who the audience was?

> Why was the subject chosen? What was the purpose of the paper?

> What subject is being discussed? Does your reader already know the facts? Are you dependent on references to authorities?

> What are the main points being presented?

> What is suggested in the conclusion?

Module III

Public Voice

Module III

Public Voice

You speak in two voices, your private voice and your public voice. This latter is the voice you use when you have something to say from your professional position. You acknowledge your public persona as student, teacher, chairman, employee, parent, voter, as a functioning member of society.

In this guise you will live in your community and, whatever your job, you will be obligated to make reports, respond to societal situation, present ideas, and influence opinions.

Every organization or group activity (PTA, church group, service club, political group) has the need for communication. You will want to reach your membership or tell strangers about your activity. The four most used avenues are: the news sheet (or group bulletin), publicity releases sent to the newspaper, those sent to radio stations, and those sent to TV stations. Each medium has special requirements which you will want to learn about.

When you studied rhetoric in Freshman English you learned ways of persuasion, but you may have forgotten that essential difference between factual presentation and persuasion. In this module we will deal with that difference. We will also look at the forms of releases which are appropriate for the various media.

Module III

Unit A

Reporting Facts

We are able to sense the difference between newspaper articles which tell the facts about an event or situation -- those statements which answer the questions: Who? Where? When? What? How? -- and those articles which are intended to arouse our reactions and persuade us to respond intellectually and emotionally.

Unit A. Assignment

Look through a newspaper until you can find a purely factual item or article. This is not going to be an easy search. Now imagine yourself in a situation in which you want to persuade your audience in favor of some attitude toward this material. Using only those facts in the original report (though not necessarily all of them), write a brief article which is slanted toward your bias. Try to write a publishable item, one which is subtly persuasive. You may want to use some of the following:

selection and omission of facts

qualifying modifiers and language devices

sarcasm, irony, other tone devices (remember, be very subtle -- newspapers will not print anything they consider non-professional)

Module III

Unit B

Newspaper Releases

Let's turn for advice on public relations to Murray Arnold, formerly the coordinator of publications and educational information for the Kern County Superintendent of Schools Office. That is a fancy way of saying that he handled the P.R. for all the schools in Kern County, including newspaper, radio, and television releases. Mr. Arnold explains here about the various areas of mass media.

    .   .   .   .   .

Mass media includes the spectrum of newspaper, radio, television, magazines; anything that communicates to the general public.

If you are going into almost any organization, you are apt to find yourself, at some point, advising people as to what is going on, informing an audience or audiences about what your organization is doing, putting its best foot forward whenever possible. But, essentially, you will be advising the public as to how your organization is functioning and its relevance to your reader.

Consider the basic precepts, the kinds of things you should keep in mind. I think primarily, in dealing with the media, you should realize that you're dealing with many publics; the taxpayers, the members of your organization, the people that support it but are not necessarily a part of the organization, and perhaps union labor, if it is something of more scope than just a church organization or a P.T.A. You will be writing to people in different walks of life. So you must keep the audience in mind before you do any writing.

But you know there is another kind of audience not reached through regular newspapers. It is reached by the kind of news sheet you get through the mail from groups you belong to. This medium requires a special kind of writing. It will be more informal than a newspaper release. Also, you will very likely use a certain jargon, one that will be understood by your members. If you're talking to educators, you could use terms such as "innovative practices," or "cognitive," or "modularized." These terms would be understood by your audience, whereas with the general public, they would not be appropriate.

There is an advantage in sending out your news in a news sheet, a house organ, as opposed to putting the news in a newspaper. The house organ is like centering in on a specific audience. If you were to put the same information in the city newspaper, it would go to a great many people who are not particularly interested. You may want to reach this wider audience, for community relations or for getting non-member support for a project.

Let us consider this larger audience. If you are going to advise people through the medium of the newspaper, your first stop, I think, would be the editor or the publisher of the newspapers. It's best to make an appointment to see these people because different newspapers and other publications, such as magazines for example, have different deadlines. It is always best to bear in mind that the editor has commitments on his time and that there are times when it would be better to talk to him when he is not under pressure. Telephone and ask for the News Editor. The News Editor would very possibly make an appointment with you if you were the publicity chairman for your organization and say come in at such and such a time and ask for so and so.

Besides talking to you, he has material he can give you to help you write publishable material right from the start.

Newspapers usually have a Guide available with helpful information for persons who do publicity work. It is like a style guide. It's very helpful because it gives information as to how newspapers handle copy.

As for special knowledge, you need first of all just the ability to write factually and coherently. So far as tools are concerned, you're going to type the copy, so you need a typewriter, and if you're going to use photographs, a camera. It's a good idea to take photos and submit them with your story.

There are simple directions for news photos. One that is basic is to make a contrasty picture. the portrait type picture is often times muddy. Make one that has high contrast. And most newspapers prefer to have people doing something instead of just looking at the camera. And most newspapers have some fairly rigid rules about the number of people. If you have 3 or 4 people, this is a good limit. Don't have them looking at the camera, but have them doing something. This adds more interest to the picture.

As for the writing, the newspaper story is written in the form of an inverted pyramid. The most important facts of the story are in the lead -- who, when, why, and how and other details. The extraneous facts can be added to the story once the lead paragraphs are written. The editor must edit from his copy in order to fit his layout. If he has to make cuts in the story, he prefers to cut it from the bottom, to take out extraneous details, the details that have a diminishing interest. He doesn't wreck the sense of the story.

How long can a news story be?

Preferably, and this is particuarly true if you are handling public relations work for an organization, make the story about a page and one-eighth, double spaced. This is referred to as a "take and a half." A "take" being about 6 inches in linotype. The sheet you write on is 8-1/2" x 11" typing paper. Inexpensive paper is preferable. Remember that a glossy finish paper, which is the expensive sort, is harder to edit. Don't try to impress anybody by using expensive paper. You should leave plenty of space at the top of the story. When the story is given a headline, this area is where the editor makes the marks that indicate the kind of a head to be run on the story. Anything that you can do to accommodate the editor is to your benefit. Editors work under tremendous pressure and the less blue-penciling and the fewer corrections they have to make in the story, the better.

There are some other special ways in which a release differs from the kind of report you had in school. It should indicate when the release can be published. Put something like "For Immediate Release" or "For Release after Mon., June 20." That goes in the upper left hand corner of the copy and it should be dated and it should have a "slug" line that indicates to the editor what this piece of copy is all about. You must give him reference material too, in that same area: the group you represent, your name, and your phone number.

Then, at the end of the first sheet, if there is one to follow, you always put "More." You must remember that an editor has a great many sheets of paper on his desk, particularly when he is working against a deadline. Then, on the last sheet, the wind up of the story, you should use the term "Thirty." It can be written out or preferably just in digits: -30-

Be sure to double space your copy, or triple space it, and of course be absolutely accurate in names and dates. Your spelling must be right -- so look up any hard words. One nice thing about form, though: in a news release you have some latitude in paragraphing that you don't have in formal English. Most newspaper paragraphs are only one sentence long. If your paragraph is too long, in type it looks like a sort of repellent area of gray. The average reader likes more white space and that is one reason there is a more casual approach to paragraphing in a news story.

There is more than one kind of a news release that a public relations person gets out.

One simply lays out the cold facts of the matter. In other stories you may be trying to persuade people to participate in something. In such a story you would use more imagination and more emphasis on comprehensive facts.

In the first you would include the place, the name of the group, the name of the kind of meeting, the place it's going to meet, when it's going to meet and maybe the fee or something like that.

In the other, besides those facts, you might give the reader some idea as to how attending the meeting or supporting the event will benefit him. You might quote one of the people involved. Now you have a human interest story. Remember, names make the news. Catch your reader's interest in the first few sentences; get him to feel that he wants to participate in what you are publicizing. Incidentally, it's a good idea, if you are going to quote somebody, to let him know what it was that he just said.

But whether you want to inform or persuade, whether you want to get into an organization news sheet or the

metropolitan newspaper my advice would be the same:
make it clean and legible, make it accurate,
interesting, and timely.

.   .   .   .   .

Here are two releases: one for a news sheet, one
for the daily newspaper. What do you feel are the main
differences between them? You will want to look at

Language level: choice of words, selection of
idioms, language tone.
Use of references: obscure or factual,
abbreviated or explained, direct quotation or
allusion.
Form: does the material follow the established
pattern of the "inverted pyramid"?

CONSUMER TAKE NOTE

Guide to the Responsible Consumer, an AAUW
publication, is available in attractive reprint form.
Read about common frauds and deceptive practices and
exactly where to turn for redress. Buy in quantity,
sell for profit -- a dandy Centennial Fund money-maker.
$.35 per copy; 101 to 600, $.15 discount. All orders
must be prepaid except for shipping and handling
charges (10% of shipping costs) which will be billed on
shipment. AAUW Sales Office, 2401 Va. Ave. NW, Wash.,
D.C. 20037.

from **AAUW Journal** August, 1973 p. 9

S C H O O L   N E W S

Newspaper release
From
Kern County Supt. of Schools
Harry E. Blair
1415 Truxtun Ave., Bakersfield
327-2111, Ex. 2651

For Immediate Release
July 5, 1972
LIFE PLANNING WORKSHOP

University of California at Santa Barbara will present a course in Kern County to combat what some observers call "the aimless pattern of modern living." The study, scheduled for July 14-16, will be called Life Planning Workshop. Instructors are a widely recognized man and wife team, Dr. and Mrs. Steward B. Shapiro of UCSB.

Enrollment deadline for the course, in which a student may earn one and one-half units of college credits, is July 11 (Tuesday).

"This is a week-end program to help people select self-fulfilling choices in the face of major life decisions. Choices," Dr. Shapiro says, "will be based on experience, and the course will utilize structured small group activities to assist participants in creating plans of strategy. The students will discover personal strengths and weaknesses; clarify life values

(more)

and goals; and delineate action steps for goal attainment."

Site of the class will be Kern View Community Health Center and Hospital, 3600 San Dimas St., Bakersfield.

Dr. Shapiro is a clinical psychologist and professor of education at UCSB. He is the author of numerous publications on psychology, and has an extensive background in personal, interpersonal, small group and organizational dynamics. Mrs. Shapiro, who has a Master of Arts degree in confluent education, has worked with her husband in workshops at UCLA, the National Training Laboratories, and at Santa Barbara.

(30)

Unit B.   Assignment

Look at the photo of the marching band.

Write two releases based on this event, one for the
news sheet of a local organization and one for the
daily newspaper. Keep in mind the specific interest of
the particular audience of each. Explain briefly what
you have done.

Module III

Unit C

Bias and Truth

One of the most persuasive media to reach us today is that of television. Almost everything we see and hear on TV is there to convince us to do something, to buy something, or to react in some specific way.

Unit C. Assignment

Select one TV viewing experience and analyze what is being done to you. Report as completely as you can about the experience:

Determine the bias of the material.

Identify the devices used to persuade you.

What was the factual content of the program or segment?

What audience was this material intended to reach?

How was it slanted to reach you?

How effective do you believe it was?

How effective would it have been if it had been presented without bias?

Module III

Unit D

Radio and TV

For advice on writing for radio and TV we will turn again to Murray Arnold, as we did in Unit B of this module.

.   .   .   .   .

Most of the things I pointed out about writing for newspapers are true of television and radio writing. It should be accurate, it should be interesting and timely. Also, you must remember, paticularly with television, that action is a necessary ingredient.

Keep in mind that radio and television copy has to be said rather than just read. The announcer must be given material that is easy to articulate. Sentences cannot be too long. They should be shorter than the average newspaper sentence if possible. Read a newspaper paragraph aloud. You'll notice "s's" are hard to articulate, so in writing for radio and TV you avoid them whenever possible.

The format of the news release for radio and television is different, too. If you remember when we were discussing newspaper copy, it's double-spaced copy. In radio and television you offer material that is written in capital letters and triple-spaced. This is more easily read by a man sitting at a desk with the copy some distance from him. The copy itself is, of course, shorter. Because of the time allotted, radio and television copy is far more condensed than newspaper copy.

Radio stations seem to be able to give longer time segments to a news release than television can, so for television keep to ten- or twenty-second spots where possible. Once in a while they can go a minute for something but the best rule to follow is to not go more than thirty seconds on a TV news story.

Now, do you know how long thirty seconds' worth of copy is? I think the usual practice (as far as I am concerned) is to write the copy first and then time it. What isn't within that time scale -- cut it; tailor it to size. Roughly ten seconds is twenty-five words, twenty is fifty words, thirty is seventy-five words and a minute about one hundred fifty for slow, clear reading. A good thing to do (this helps the announcer) is to put in the upper right hand corner the number of seconds that this copy takes.

Radio and television stations are generous about giving public service time and running organizational news that is acceptable -- it should be interesting, of course.

As in newspaper copy, you put in when it is to be released, date it is submitted, who is sending it, and what we call a slug-line (even in radio) which indicates something about the story itself.

The same thing is true of television copy insofar as identification of the copy; however the format is quite different. With a ruler and pencil you can make your own television copy paper by indicating that the left half is the visual material and the right half is the audio. The visual column describes the slide you're submitting to go with your copy. The first slide is identified as "Slide no. 1" and underneath it you write a descriptive phrase. That means to the program director or the people behind the camera that this is the slide that goes in this position. The copy which is typed opposite the slide number and description is the material which goes with that particular slide. Slide no. 2 and no. 3 will be treated the same way. A release designed for one minute would probably take three slides.

Slides are quite easy to make. An inexpensive camera will make good color slides. One word of caution: you should shoot your scene as a horizontal rather than a vertical. Often, one slide is enough. It depends somewhat on the length of the story you're presenting. Remember that the announcer or program director may want to cut this copy. And here again the copy is written in such a way that he can cut from the bottom. He can do away with some of your slides, he can do away with some of the copy and just go with the first paragraph. Sometimes there is great advantage in having a slide rear-projected back of the announcer, and it can remain on all the time that he is functioning in front of the microphone. The program director will make that decision -- he is the boss. The announcer is sometimes program director as well.

65

It's a good idea to contact someone in radio and television before sending in releases. Television people are quite generous about public service time and oftentimes they will make suggestions that will be immensely helpful. They have people on their staffs as a rule who will write the copy for you in case you are not a writer, if you simply present them with the facts.

You may want to handle the whole thing with a fact sheet. That's a bare outline of the story itself. It gives material that will help the announcer. Perhaps he will find himself with a few spare seconds. He can look at a fact sheet and add a little something to the story. The fact sheet is useful, too, if he's going to turn it over to a copy writer.

The fact sheet is handy in another area. If the television station is going to send a camera man out on an assignment and there isn't time for you to get together with a program director, you can hand a fact sheet to the camera man and the reporter who's assigned to the story. This gives them valuable ammunition to use in a show they're going to present later on. I believe the most important rules to follow in public relations are very simple. Remember that you are communicating with many publics, not just the church group, not just the P.T.A., but many people will be in your audience. And be a good listener as well as a communicator. You can often make a much more effective presentation if you have been receptive to two-way communication.

Radio release

From   1-min.
Kern County Supt. of Schools
Harry E. Blair
1415 Truxtun Ave., Bakersfield
327-2111, Ex. 2651

For Immediate Release
July 6, 1972
MARINE BIOLOGY CLASSES

MARINE BIOLOGY COURSES WILL BE OFFERED AT MORRO BAY THIS SUMMER BY CAL STATE BAKERSFIELD, THE COUNTY SUPERINTENDENT OF SCHOOLS, AND NATIONAL SCIENCE FOUNDATION. THE SIX-WEEK PROGRAM WILL CONSIST OF LESSONS IN TIDE POOLS AND SEA FORMS GEOLOGY, AND CHAPARRAL. COLLEGE CREDIT WILL BE AVAILABLE. INSTRUCTORS ARE SCIENTISTS UNDER DIRECTION OF DOCTOR JOHN COASH OF CAL STATE BAKERSFIELD. MOST CLASSES WILL BE NEAR MORRO BAY.

THE FEE OF TWO HUNDRED DOLLARS WILL INCLUDE TUITION, ROOM AND BOARD. ENROLLMENT IS OPEN TO ANYONE, BUT IS SPECIALLY GEARED TO TEACHERS WITH A LIMITED SCIENCE BACKGROUND. DATES OF THE COURSE ARE FROM JULY FIRST TO AUGUST FIFTEENTH; TRANSPORTATION WILL BE FURNISHED. THE SCHOOL AT MORRO BAY IS ABOUT ONE HUNDRED AND FIFTY MILES FROM BAKERSFIELD. ENROLLMENT DEADLINE IS JUNE TWENTIETH.

(END)

67

Television Release

From   30-sec.
Kern County Supt. of Schools
Harry E. Blair
1415 Truxtun Ave., Bakersfield
327-2111, Ex. 2651

For Immediate Release
July 6, 1972

VISUAL   AUDIO

SLIDE No. 1   MARINE BIOLOGY IS ONE OF MANY

(view of Morro   SUBJECTS OFFERED THIS SUMMER IN

Bay)   CLASSES NEAR MORRO BAY. SPONSORS

                          ARE CAL STATE BAKERSFIELD, THE

                          COUNTY SUPERINTENDENT OF SCHOOLS,

                          AND   THE   NATIONAL   SCIENCE

                          FOUNDATION.

SLIDE No. 2   THE SIX-WEEK PROGRAM GIVES COLLEGE

(students by   CREDIT   FOR   NOMINAL   TUITION.

the sea)   TEACHING WILL BE INFORMAL BUT

                          THOROUGH WITH EXPERT SCIENTISTS IN

                          CHARGE OF SMALL GROUPS. IT WILL

                          BE BIOLOGY TAUGHT IN NATURE'S OWN

                          CLASSROOMS OF SEA AND SURF.

SLIDE No. 3   FOR FURTHER INFORMATION CALL CAL

(CSB logo)   STATE COLLEGE BAKERSFIELD.

Unit D. Assignment

Radio and TV releases differ from publicity intended to be read. Study the sample releases included with this unit. Now, think of an event which might be covered by the media in a public service spot (an activity of some club or non-profit organization, an event on campus, an open meeting with some well known speaker). Write two releases on the same subject, one for radio, one for TV. Be direct and factual, try to inform as well as interest. But remember to be persuasive, too. Be sure to use the forms which radio and TV stations prefer. Indicate the length of time you expect these spots to take. Below are the only time slots used in the media.

Both in radio and TV
    25 words make a 10-second spot
    50 words make a 20-second spot
    75 words make a 30-second spot
    150 words make a one-minute spot

Follow the form used here; these are standard forms.

At the end, add a note (not for broadcast) which explains what audience you are appealing to.

Module IV

Letter Writing

Module IV

Letter Writing

Before you begin to write a letter, ask yourself this simple question: "Why am I writing this letter?" If the answer comes to you clearly and succinctly, chances are your letter will be direct, easy to understand, effective. And chances are too that you will elicit the response you are after.

Set about the task of letter writing as you would set about doing any other job. Get the equipment lined up. Think out what you are about to do. Get your audience clearly in mind. Then get the job done.

The main point about equipment is that it be appropriate. You do not want the paper, ink, or script to be so overpowering that the recipient forgets to pay attention to the message. Remember, you are in control of the situation; be sure you get the kind of reaction you are after. Shock has its place, whimsy its appeal. But when you are seeking a serious intelligent response write a serious intelligent letter. Generally speaking the standard kind of equipment has become accepted as standard because it allows the reader to give full attention to what you are saying.

White or off-white paper shows off writing most effectively. Black or blue-black ink (or typewriter ribbon) is most easily deciphered. If you allow a margin of an inch or an inch and a half both left and right, with even more white space top and bottom, you

73

give the reader chance for maximum concentration.

It goes without saying that the writing itself must be legible. Type for greatest clarity. If you have a nice clear handwriting, that is good too. But if your written line looks like never-ending wavelets with occasional airborne doughnuts to indicate a dotted i, then be sure to print in nice elementary-school capitals anything which is factual and important.

While we are on the subject of appropriate language for specific needs, there are a few generalities worth saying. Keep your language plain and direct -- no cliches, no businessese, no jargon of the rushed executive. Let the tone fit the need. Whenever you can, try to imagine the situation and possible mood of the person to whom you are writing. Anger and irritation are not likely to bring about much positive action in your favor. On the other hand, most people like to associate with those who show a little vitality and purpose. After all, the letter you send is a fragment of yourself. It represents you -- it is you.

The keywords for success are the same ones which apply to all communication: be brief enough to avoid boring, complete enough to satisfy the receiver's interest. Be accurate. What is down in writing is there to substantiate your thoughts. And it is there to be referred to as long as the paper lasts.

Sometimes, in an effort to be effective, a writer is tempted to belabor a point. At other times emotional reaction will cause a writer to mis-identify what the whole problem is all about. So in letter writing, as in other forms of communication, it is to your benefit if you can allow a cooling-off period between the initial writing and the effective moment when the recipient gets your message. You need not lose that fresh human feeling which impulse writing has. But before you lick the flap on the envelope, check to see that the facts are all included. And that the mixture is not any richer than one part emotion to two parts reason.

Now you face the need for your letter. After you have answered that first "why?" question as you pull together the effective points of argument (if it is going to be that kind of letter) or your particular needs (if it is that kind), you have probably worked out an attention-getting opening and main part of the letter. But before you get too far along in the process, ask yourself the second question: "What do I want the recipient to do about this?" The best kind of letter is like the best kind of one-speaker's-turn in a dialogue. As you finish your part you hand over the initiative to the other person. It is like tossing a ball. Give the other person the opportunity for response.

Now to begin with, there really are not any hard and fast rules about letter writing. The post office has some definite rules about how you address an envelope and what size object it is willing to handle. Inside the envelope you are on your own. Courtesy, clarity, legibility -- those concepts are easily seen. The most effective device you can use, the most universally persuasive, is the tone you employ.

A negative approach automatically arouses antipathy. Accusation, attack, threats, and anger are less effective than reasonable explanations and forthright requests. It is true that a good verbal blast may be good therapy for the blaster. If it is therapy you want -- go to it. But if your idea is to get something accomplished, tear up the blast and send out a reasonable second try. You do not have to become obsequious. Just think about how you would react if you were receiving the letter.

A word about vocabulary. As you well know by now, an understanding of your audience gives you a particular level of language in which you will write. But even though your readers may be wielders of the perfected cliche, show them that you can communicate as one human being to another, not as one computer to another. "Yours of the inst received" and "to facilitate, effectuate, and finalize" have the appeal of an obscure aboriginal dialect, but they do not get the job done. Write as you speak -- or rather, write as you speak when everything is going just right for you.

76

Module IV

Unit A

Letter of Application

One kind of letter which plays an important part in your life is the letter of application, specifically a job application. It sometimes seems as though there is something mystic about a good one, but actually there are a few acknowledged strong points in a good application which can be easily learned.

Again, as in all writing, the first and most important question must be asked: who is your audience? When you can imagine the best possible reception that your letter can get, you will also be able to imagine what that letter should sound like. You will know the language level which will be most effective, you will limit what you say to what is needed, and you will regulate your tone.

Every letter is a small sample of yourself, but the letter of application is more. It is an emissary to send ahead to prepare the way for your own coming. So in this case, two special people are involved in an effective contact within that letter: you and the recipient. You are going to be neat and orderly to demonstrate your own character. You are going to be brief and direct out of respect for the busy professional life of the other person. You are going to be sincere because this is not the time for fooling anybody.

77

PENINSULA COLLEGE LIBRARY
PORT ANGELES WASHINGTON

But what are you going to say?

Custom suggests that your first contact with a prospective employer should be factually accurate and complete. If you send a resume of your past education and experience, plus a covering letter, the recipient will be able to study your background before you meet one another. Then you will be able to talk together about your particular talents and abilities.

First, the resume. There is no authorized form for this information, but the following pattern is one which has proved effective. It should be typed on regular sized typing paper, single spaced but blocked for easy reading, neat, clear, and in chronological order. Usually the most recent events come first, moving progressively (if that is the word for it) back in time. On the top of the page put your most needed data: your name, address, phone number, and date, and, if it is appropriate, the kind of job you are applying for. Probably your background falls into two categories, your experience and your education. If so, begin with the subhead EXPERIENCE and list your present job, its job description (or at any rate what you do now which would help in getting the job you are applying for), the dates you have held the job, the name of your immediate superior (who should be warned that someone may ask about you). Now list the job you had prior to this one and include the same information. Continue this back to the date you came out of school. If you have had only summer or part-time work, list it in this same fashion. If you have done volunteer work which is similar to the professional job you are seeking, put that in, too.

Now you are ready for the second category, EDUCATION. Under this heading list the places where you have studied, and again list the most recent place first.

Many people believe a one-page resume is best. Personally, I think what you include is more important than the page count. But do not go over two pages. A resume is, by definition, short.

The resume is like a formal studio portrait of you in your professional guise. The covering letter is like a snapshot -- but it is still you the professional, not you on a holiday weekend. So the covering letter will be sincere, brief, and informative. It will give the pertinent facts too -- who you are, why you are writing, and what is attached (the resume). Tell here why you feel you are especially right for the job.

Your tone will be business-like but pleasant, and you will state in this letter what you want the recipient to do: tell him that you are hoping for an appointment for an interview, and you may want to suggest that you will telephone to make that appointment.

This letter, like the resume, should be typed on standard sized white typewriter paper. You are contributing material for your own personnel file. It is going to be with you a long time. What seems bright and interesting and unusual to you now may seem childish and contrived a few years from now -- and might even seem that way to others right now. On the whole, a letter in your most dignified style is best at this point, not stilted or pompous, but in keeping with the job you are seeking.

There are times when an imaginative and freak application is called for, something daringly different. But you will know when that time comes by the way in which the job opening is announced. Like all other communication, the job offer and response are part of a two-way negotiation. Let the employer set the tone. If your ingenuity is being tested, the ad will show it. Let your answer echo the tone of the question. It sets the style, you follow through.

Checklist for letters of application

on time with your original letter and your follow-up (and of course punctual for your interview)

on target with effective words that go right to the heart of the matter

all-inclusive with names, dates, addresses, and other vital facts

accurate and carefully proof-read to insure the communication of what you mean to communicate

balanced in length: long enough to be comprehensive yet brief enough to hold the reader

attractive in appearance: neat, clean, and orderly in its organization

Form for resume

Your name, address, city, state, zip   phone

EXPERIENCE

    Current job, company or school   date hired
    address   "to present"
    job description
    supervisor

    Previous job, company, or school   date hired
    address   and ending
    job description   date
    supervisor
    etc.

EDUCATION

    Institution, location   degree earned   date
    College, location   degree earned   date
    High School, location   date
    (include any special awards or honors)

REFERENCES

    Here list three respected professional persons,
    addresses, city, state, zip (not listed above).
    Choose people who know your quality as a working
    person.

(Keep all dates in an orderly column on the right.
Neatness counts!)

(This, though fictional and foolish, demonstrates how a resume might look.)

JANE EYRE, Moor House, Marsh End near Morton, Yorkshire	333-1848

EXPERIENCE

Resident teacher, Morton School Supervise elementary studyhall, teach math, writing, embroidery, water coloring Ref.: Rev. St. J. Rivers	Jan. 1808 to date
Private tutor, Thornfield Hall, Millcote, Yorkshire Complete charge of education of first-grade student. Emphasis on reading and the arts. Ref.: Mr. E. F. Rochester	Jan. 1807 to Jan. 1808
Elementary teacher, Lowood School Assisted all teachers with activities for resident students. Developed program which emphasized humility and decorum Ref.: Mr. Brocklehurst	Sept. 1805 to Jan. 1807

EDUCATION

Lowood School, Yorkshire Teacher-training program including: prayers, scripture-reading, recitations, history, grammar, writing, and arithmetic. Special award in Survival Tactics.	Jan. 1779 to Sept. 1805

REFERENCES

Ms. Diana Rivers, Moor House, Marsh End near Morton, Yorkshire

Ms. Maria Temple, Mistress, Lowood School, Yorks.

Mr. Henry Biggs, Solicitor, Temple Inn, London

There is a certain order in the way most hiring is handled. There is an opening and word of it reached you (through a newspaper ad, a posted letter of announcement, word of mouth, information from a placement agency -- or one of many other ways). If you are interested, you respond with your resume and covering letter. You follow-up by phoning for an appointment. You have the interview as scheduled. And, no matter what they said that they were going to do, be sure you follow up with a letter. Now that you and the interviewer have met, have had personal contact, the tone of your follow-up letter can be more informal and more personal than your earlier letter. But remember above all, the purpose of your letter is to express thanks for the interview to show that you came away from the meeting still wanting the job. Remember, too, who you are (a professional speaking to another professional about the serious matter of a career). So **audience** and **purpose** will again control your tone.

But how about the job possibility that you initiate? It is true that not all jobs are listed and posted. At times a company may feel the need for a new person and yet not get around to doing anything about it. Or sometimes they have enough applications coming in unsolicited that they forego the announcement. How can you get your name in for a job like that?

Well, to start with, you have to think of the job. Then you must write a letter to a decision-maker in the company suggesting that it would be to his advantage to talk to you. Usually this person will be the president. In any case, start at the top. All your skill with language and your natural charm must come to your aid.

Say first why you are writing -- why you believe that particular organization should consider you. Say why you want to work there. Introduce yourself by stating what there is about you or your background which fits you for a job with this company. Attach your resume. Suggest that you will call Tuesday (or some specific day) to set up an appointment for an interview. And then do so, with the same confident positive attitude you showed in the letter.

But stay buoyant. If there is no opening, thank whomever you talk to and send your letter to other firms. Remember, there is a right job for you. Just hang on until the opening and your application and the successful interview all work out together.

Unit A. Assignment

Think of the job you would most like to have (invent one if one does not exist). Holding to the true facts about yourself, prepare a formal letter of application and include an accurate resume.

Module IV

Unit B

Business Letter

In writing to a business firm or a service company, let your need set the tone. If something is broken or you need professional assistance, you may feel an urgency, but we will assume that in an emergency you have already dealt with these people by phone or in person. Chances are that when you get to the letter-writing stage you have reached a pitch of action which has you eager for results. Now, how can you get them?

First, get your letter to the right person. If you have no idea who is in charge, go to the top. There is a lot to be said for addressing the president directly. Your letter may not get there (presidents are world famous for having protecting secretaries and executive assistants) but your complaint will probably be deflected toward the best person to handle the affair. There is much to be said for writing to someone who appears to be in charge, with a line at the bottom of the letter which reports: "copy to Charles C. Brown, President." And do send President Brown a copy. Maybe that bottom line does as much good as the copy, but go all the way.

You may be dealing with a computer. Computers never get angry. But they also cannot be wheedled into a sympathetic position as they do not reason beyond their own preconceived pattern. If you should begin one of those deplorable never-ending and non-varying correspondences with the subscription department computer or the one at the monthly book or record club, you have only one way out. Be factual, act the part of a twelve-digit account number and not a person, supply insistently only the information for which the computer has a slot, and develop long-standing patience. Finally, when you despair of action, try to attract the attention of the mail distributor by an outrageous opening sentence (something amusing but stopping). Remember, every computer has a master: in serious cases it is just a question of finding him.

Beyond seeing that your letter gets to the right person, your main concern must be to see that it gets read and produces action. Make your letter easy to read. This means white standard sized letter paper (regular typing paper is ideal) and clearly written words. And again the typewriter is best. You are competing with dozens of other letter writers for the executive's time. Make your letter easy to read. Wide margins, neat paragraphs, short sentences, explicit words: here are your most appealing tools. Check again on the important words after you have sketched out your rough copy. Do they mean exactly what you want them to mean? Most words have several meanings. Are your sentences free of ambiguity?

Make your letter easy to understand. In the upper right hand corner put your address and the date. Down a few lines, above the salutation, left margin, put the name and title, and address, of the person to receive the letter. Begin "Dear Miss/Mrs./Dr./Mr. ----." Identify yourself right away: ("a customer for more than ten years," "the tenant in 2B, 1918 Delancy Place," "president of the local Ecologists Society"), and state how you can be reached both by mail and by phone.

When you have clearly identified yourself, state your problem or complaint as specifically. Give names and dates, model number and product trade name, names and addresses of any others involved. These are the facts that your addressee is interested in, facts which will help in any investigation to be activated.

Now the final point: What do you want done? You are not always going to be definite; sometimes a request that "adjustments are made" will satisfy both of you. But if this is a problem with an obvious solution ("ship me the following items C.O.D.") or ("as I have returned the merchandise please credit my account" or "please see that my name is removed from your mailing list"), say so.

As for tone, assume until it is otherwise demonstrated that this is to be a friendly adult relationship from which both of you are going to profit in the long run. You are not angry and you are not trying to make anyone else angry.

This section is built upon the presumption of a justified complaint. Of course, you will deal with businesses and services for other reasons. The same basic rules apply, however, no matter what the communication: be neat, brief, explicit; use names, dates, addresses, trade-names, model numbers; state your involvement and what you want done; be human and courteous. Yes, we all remember to complain -- but do you congratulate for extraordinary achievement? Do you let the boss know when an employee has gone out of the way to solve a difficult problem or to help you in a moment of trouble? This might be the most important letter you ever wrote, not for you but for someone worth commending.

There is no need for you to learn business terms to deal with business people. In fact, more and more companies are sending out all their correspondence in standard English, sounding now like one human being addressing another. But they remain specific and factual, using explicit nouns, action verbs, descriptive adjectives. The clue to successful business letters is simple: let the factual content of the communication over-ride the personality of the sender. You are not out to make a friend: you are one benign human being writing to another with some kind of constructive idea in mind. Put all your skill and attention on the main action.

Unit B. Assignment

We do not have to make up grievances. We all know some service (public or private) which could be improved. Write a letter which you feel would be well received and might actually bring about needed improvements.

Be specific: name models, give account numbers, explain exactly what is wrong.

Be positive: what do you expect your reader to do?

Be polite: another human being is receiving your letter; chances are, the person is not the one who caused the problem, but maybe the one who can set things straight.

Module IV

Unit C

Letter of Request

One day it will fall your lot to write a letter to someone you admire or someone whose name has been recommended to you, asking that person to speak before your group or in some other way be of service to you. All the diplomacy you have acquired will be needed if you are going to get a favorable answer. How will you handle it? First, as to tone, be very light-handed in your flattery. People being asked for favors are suspicious of insincere praise. Yes, you want to say that here is the perfect person for the job you have in mind, and you want to show how great it will be if you get "yes" as the answer. Be enthusiastic, but easy on the blarney.

As to content, be factual. State when and where, how long you have allotted for the speech, what kind of group it is, who else may be there. Announce if there is going to be an honorarium or any pay, or if the honor will have to suffice. Give information about the background and beliefs of the group so your speaker knows what he or she is in for. Say how to reach you to accept, and be sure to give a deadline, one that will give you time to find replacement if one is needed.

After the presentation to your group, be as prompt and pleasant in sending your thank-you letter.

90

In your professional life as well as your social life you too are going to receive requests -- to be a speaker, a judge, a chairman, a worker. Some of these requests you will want to accept, some you will refuse. In every case keep in mind that there is some sort of honor in the designation. They thought of you; you are the one they want.

Now when you write your letter of acceptance, keep that in mind. Be prompt in your response. Be sincere in your thanks for the honor. Repeat the facts: time, date, subject, function. This eliminates error caused by typos. If there is any question about what is expected of you, ask it now. It is good to have a friendly understanding with the person who invites you.

If you are going to refuse the request, your letter must be even more carefully written. Courteous regret is the order of the day. Be sure to convey the idea that your refusal has nothing to do with the quality of the group. Personal P.R. (everyman's own public relations) should cause you to think of yourself objectively. Ask yourself: does this letter leave the way open for further association with this group? Or, if that is the last thing you want, does the letter show you as a good person, but just not right for them?

There is another kind of request you may be called on to respond to: the letter of recommendation. Here common sense will guide you as to content. In a straightforward no-nonsense tone give clear and concise statements about the person in question. First, list as many good points as you can which relate directly to the needs of the recommendation. You are required to give truthful, pertinent, succinct, and considered answers. You should tell how long you have known the person and what kind of relationship yours has been. You might refer to any areas which you feel could be improved, particularly when you can indicate that progress is being made. However, if you feel that you must say extremely negative things about the person, then do not agree to give the recommendation. Talk to the person and suggest that someone else should write the letter. In the long run, everybody will benefit.

In all letters of this type -- request, acceptance, refusal, recommendation -- the tone is of primary importance. These are professional letters. In them, you are functioning in your capacity as a specialist. Pomposity is dreadful, but dignity fitting. This does not mean that you should try to be something you are not; it does not mean that you have to sound stuffy. But you have been asked for your opinion or service. Keep alive that feeling that you are the best one for the task. And do try, in spite of duty or dignity, to sound like a human being when you write. This quality is the prime secret of the good letter writer. Look at the letter which the editor Maxwell Perkins wrote refusing a request.

Feb. 9, 1945

Dear Mr. Cowden:

I fully appreciate the compliment of being asked to be one of the judges of the Hopwood Fiction Contest, but I must, with deep regret, decline. It is my conviction that an editor should be even more obscure than a child, who should be seen. The editor should be neither seen nor heard, or so I think. And so I have made it a rule to do nothing but the regular editorial work, and not speak, or lecture, or act as a judge, or to take on anything on the outside, even when greatly tempted, as now.

Ever sincerely yours,

Maxwell Perkins

from **Editor to Author: The Letters of Maxwell E. Perkins**, p. 264

Unit C. Assignment

You have been assigned the task of getting a speaker for some group you are with (at least for the purpose of this assignment). Write a letter which will influence that speaker in your favor.

Now, suppose such a letter had been sent to you. Write a second letter, this one refusing to speak but still staying on good terms with the group.

Module IV

Unit D

Friendly Letters

There is only one simple principle to keep in mind when you write a friendly letter: be yourself. A letter to someone you know, someone you care for, is like a visit. You will not know, until you receive the answer, how your friend responds to what you are saying. But except for that time-lag between question and answer, comment and reaction, you are talking person to person.

The tone of the letter controls your interpersonal relationship. Subconsciously you are moving forward in your understanding of each other, and your primary effort, as in daily conversation, is to maintain an easy flow of ideas. Your second natural attempt is to reveal more about yourself, your actions and thoughts, which will advance the level of your friendship. You are calling to mind ideas you agree upon, experiences you have shared, mutual friends and areas of interests. You are introducing new thoughts, ideas, experiences with the hope that this friend will respond and reveal new and interesting things. If you want to get an immediate answer, ask a direct question. We are all roused to reply when we feel that our private knowledge is being applied to.

All of our friends do not exist on the same level of understanding. Instinctively we know how revealing we intend to be with various friends. No one can tell you how casual you should be with a friend. You alone know whether your language level is slang and colloquial, an in-language. You alone know the most appropriate subject matter. You alone know how open and self-exposing you are going to be. But remember that, whatever the level, this is the real you functioning in a highly personal relationship. And here -- as in all areas of writing -- you are functioning on a special level designed to meet the needs of a special audience.

Unit D. Assignment

Now, as a demonstration of this principle, try this:

Something pleasant has just happened in your personal life: write about it in three short friendly letters (1) to an older member of your family, (2) to a close friend, and (3) to someone out of your past whom you respect (a former teacher, your boss, your minister, an older friend).

Module V

Words, Words, Words

Module V

Words, Words, Words

Why do we have rules about writing? Why can't we just write the way we feel like writing?

Conventions are habits of behavior which create a meeting ground for understanding. There is a difference between restriction which inhibits and that which stabilizes, between liberty which is disorganized and that which is disciplined. As we need mutual understanding in order to communicate, we must accept some mutually advantageous discipline. Traditional spelling and consistent grammar make communication easier. Without this consistency, chaos would take over.

In fact, it was not until printing was developed that people felt the need for some system of prescribed spelling. Before that, when you received a letter from a friend, you accepted the challenge to interpret some pretty rough approximations of what your friend thought a word sounded like. It might have been fun, but it certainly was not efficient.

So now you can turn to a dictionary when you are in doubt of what standard spelling is. But for your way of putting words together in serviceable pattern and sequence, you will depend on your basic understanding of your own native tongue. Most of us do not have an English language-learning background which includes learning formal rules. Many did not have to diagram sentences or conjugate and decline English words. As very young children we learned through speaking, through communicating with our parents and other young children.

Unfortunately, we may have picked up some speech habits which worked very well in childhood, but are not effective in our present situation. Also, as we grew older and more rushed and harried, we added a few careless errors and new expressions of jargon and slang which are not appropriate in standard or general English. Whatever is not conventionally understood detracts from the clarity of communication.

Words are symbols. The most reliable word will signal to your reader the meaning which you intended to convey. The best word to use is one which is accurate, necessary, and evocative of the appropriate meaning. Fancy and unusual words do not improve understanding. Here is a single-sentence statement of purpose worded by a committee for a state board of higher education. What happened to sense?

The purpose of this project is to develop the capability for institutions of higher learning and community agencies and organizations to coalesce for the development of community services and create a model for the coordination of such services that would maximize the available resources from a number of institutions and provide communication and priority needs and the responses of the educational needs of a given community.

Simple, direct, straightforward writing is almost always the easiest to understand and therefore the most effective communication.

In a similar manner, the basic cluster of words, the sentence (subject + verb + object if needed) is best when it is clear, evocative of thought, and natural in cadence, appealing to the mind and to the inner ear. If we remember the audience, if we are aware of the particular interests and limitations of our selected audience, chances are that we will write clearly and effectively.

Module V

Unit A

Recognizing Word Power

Although most people have never considered it, the most valued word in a sentence is the verb. The next most influential ones are the nouns. Adjectives and adverbs are a long way down on the list.

First, about nouns: if we were to be limited to one axiom for the student it should be: be specific! In your first version, the first intuitive outpouring, use the first word that occurs to you. But go back later and substitute the one word which is indispensable in each particular case. Search diligently until you locate the exact noun which suits your need.

There are specific nouns and general nouns to designate anything. Consider this ladder of specification:

"Jade"
beagle
hound
dog
canine
quadraped
mammal
animal

Each level is more specific than the one below it. You must decide which level best expresses your idea. Sometimes a noun must be modified to make it more specific.

Nouns have another level of appeal: there are denotative nouns and connotative ones and some which may be either, depending on the usage. A denotative noun explicates or designates. A connotative noun implies an abstract meaning beyond the one which it designates. Consider the difference between the meaning of **house** and **home**, **average** and **mediocre**, **willing** and **unresisting**, **relative** and **mother**.

Be sure you are aware of the overtones evoked by the words you select.

When you select a verb, be aware of the aura it carries with it. If you say, "I will succeed," you give a very different message than when you say, "I will not fail."

Mark Twain's advice was, "As to the adjective, when in doubt, strike it out." We cannot eliminate modifiers from our language, but if we are careful in our choice of nouns and verbs, we will depend less and elss on supporting modifiers.

Unit A. Assignment

Try out some special words. In a descriptive paragraph, reveal an action which you recently witnessed (for example: a play in some sport; a meeting of two people; the simple human activity of unlocking a car, opening a package, running the photocopy machine).

Now: go through your passage and underline all the modifying words, all the adjectives and adverbs. Rewrite the passage eliminating as many of these modifiers as you can. You will have to use more vital verbs and more specific nouns to keep the passage as informative as it was.

Now: go through the passage and underline all the nouns. Are these as specific and connotative as any you could have chosen? If not, write the passage again with more carefully chosen nouns.

Finally go through the revised passages and put a box around each verb. Here are the words which give strength to your passage. Change any which you think could be improved. Make your verbs work. Select verbs which have auras, which send out special vibes. If you are making a positive statement, use strong positive verbs. Now compare this final version with the first one. Any improvement?

Module V

Unit B

Using Basics

Perhaps you have never considered the force of the most ordinary aspects of language. We follow certain conventions in serious writing because they have proved to be forceful and highly understandable. One convention concerns tense. Stories are retold in the present tense: Hamlet is indecisive; Don Quixote tilts at windmills. No matter how many times we open the book, the protagonist is still doing what the author arranged for him to do. Novels are generally written in the past tense. Why? Because this tense has proved to be the most acceptable to the reader.

Certain tenses seem to be of a family and are used together: **is-can-will-may** make one sequence; **was-could-would-might** form another. We follow these traditional patterns because they are most acceptable to most readers.

But there are other aspects of tense which are more subtle. When we write in the past tense we tell the readers about something apart from themselves. When we use the present tense we involve them directly in the action--it is as though they were here too, when it is all happening. A judicious mixing of the tenses creates an emotional involvement. Here is an example of excellence in the handling of language.

From Bocca di Magra to Bocca d'Arno, mile after mile, the sandy beaches smoothly, unbrokenly extend. Inland from the beach, behind a sheltering belt of pines, lies a strip of coastal plain—flat as a slice of Holland and dyked with slow streams. Corn grows here and the vine, with plantations of slim poplars interspersed, and fat water-meadows. Here and there the streams brim over into shallow lakes, whose shores are fringed with sodden fields of rice. And behind this strip of plain, four or five miles from the sea, the mountains rise, suddenly and steeply: the Apuan Alps (p. 9).

•   •   •   •   •

It was in this sea that he sailed his flimsy boat, steering with one hand and holding in the other his little volume of Aeschylus. You picture him so on the days of calm. And on the day of sudden violent storm you think of him, too. The lightnings cut across the sky, the thunders are like terrible explosions over-head, the squall comes down with a fury. What news of the flimsy boat? None, save only that a few days after a storm a young body is washed ashore, battered, unrecognizable; the little Aeschylus in the coat pocket is all that tells us that this was Shelley (p. 10-11).

Aldous Huxley
"On the Margin"

106

Unit B. Assignment

Write a brief explanation of what you feel is special about these two paragraphs (the opening and closing ones) from this essay by Aldous Huxley.

Look at the overall pattern of the paragraphs. In what way are they similar? Is the author dealing primarily with time or with space? What does the general pattern of progression or sequence suggest?

In the second paragraph, how has Huxley used tense to control the reader? What device has he used to move us from the past to the present? Is the first verb in the present tense a special verb in relation to time? What response do we have to that final verb in the past tense?

How has the author handled person: third person (it, he, she, they) as contrasted with first person (I or we) and second person (you)? Why does he make this shift?

How are singulars and plurals used in the first paragraph?

Two unusual plurals, "lightnings" and "thunders," appear in this second paragraph. Can you imagine what effect these plurals have on the reader?

Module V

Unit C

Check for Clarity

Intelligent communication depends on mutual understanding: you know something you want to tell people and they want to learn from you. Great. That is communication at its best. Now let us acknowledge that grammatical clarity (that is, conformation with certain conventions) is going to make it easier for everyone. Here are a few truths worth remembering before you hand your written communication to anyone:

1. Verbs agree with their subjects. (You say, "Naturally." But remember that no matter what comes between subject and verb, they still agree.)

2. A pronoun always refers back to the last mentioned noun "with which it agrees in case, number, and gender."

   Confusing: The man told the boy that he was sorry he was late. (The boy was both sorry and late.)

   The man told the boy that he was glad to meet him. (Who was glad?)

   Confusing: If the dog barks at the baby, tie it up. (The baby?)

Better: Tie up the dog if it barks at the baby.

Worst: If the dog barks at the baby, beat it. (Get going?)

When the pronoun is far removed from its antecedent, the reader may become confused.

3. Whatever modifer goes before the subject must modify it. Sometimes we want to vary our sentences and decide to invert one--that is, put a modifer (word, phrase, or clause) as the first element, preceding the subject. That makes an interesting sentence; but watch out.

Misleading: Coming around the corner, the courthouse was seen.

Better: Coming around the corner, we saw the courthouse.

Confusing: To think clearly, some logic is important.

Better: To think clearly, **you** should learn logic.

Confusing: On her first free day, she said she would phone him.

Better: She said she would phone him on her first free day.

Confusing: When frightened, his hair bristled.

Better: When he was frightened, his hair bristled.

109

4. Does it matter what pronoun you use in making editorial comments in a paper? Yes it does. Readers react predictably when they are addressed in various ways. If a writer frequently says "I," his interest is more subjective than analytical. If a writer says "you," he has set out to be instructive. If a writer says "we," he is trying to link himself with you, possibly attempting to destroy your natural resistance to his idea. If he says "one," he is affecting an imitation of British writers.

Write about the subject rather than about either writer or reader. Consider these sentences:

> It makes me sick to see boys fighting.
> (What interests me? Myself.)
> You shouldn't fight. (or) Don't fight.
> (talking down)
> We aren't going to have any more fighting, are we? (ugh)
> One doesn't fight in school. (detached)

5. The verb to be is a special verb. Vital verbs create persuasive sentences. Ordinarily, to be is the blandest, most ineffectual verb you can use. Occasionally it may serve a special need. When you want a non-assertive verb or a basically elemental one, to be answers your need.

When you do use this linking verb (or similar verbs such as **to appear, to seem, to become**) remember that it always forms the equal sign in an equation: The lawyer is my uncle (laywer = uncle). These verbs, as well as verbs of the senses (**to look, to smell, to taste, to sound, to feel**) show a relationship between the subject and a noun or a modifying adjective. "She seems timid." "The bell sounds sweet." The subject is linked to a complement, a word which completes the thought; predicate nouns rename the subject; predicate adjectives modify the subject.

You can learn a good deal from writing which is nothing like your own style. Quality supercedes vogue.

Here is a passage from the novel **Frankenstein** by Mary Shelley. Contrary to anything you may have seen in the popular comedy-horror films for kids, **Frankenstein** is a serious novel, dealing with the question: what would happen if an inexperienced living creature, totally without a knowledge of good and evil, were turned loose in the world? The answer comes back loud and clear: chaos.

This passage is taken from the narrative being related by the experimenter himself, Dr. Frankenstein. He has now regretted his audacity in creating life and is in the process of disposing of the collected miscellany which would have gone into the creation of a second creature.

As you read the passage, keep in mind the elements of time and place. The work was published in 1818 and the author was not American, but British. The passage, however, has universal appeal.

.   .   .   .   .

Between two and three in the morning the moon rose and I then, putting my basket aboard a little skiff, sailed out about four miles from the shore. The scene was perfectly solitary. A few boats were returning towards land, but I sailed way from them. I felt as if I was about the commission of a dreadful crime, and avoided with shuddering anxiety my encounter with my fellow-creatures. At one time the moon, which had before been clear, was suddenly overspread by a thick cloud and I took advantage of the moment of darkness, and cast my basket into the sea. I listened to the gurgling sound as it sunk, and then sailed away from the spot. The sky became clouded, but the air was pure, although chilled by the northeast breeze that was then rising. But it refreshed me, and filled me with such agreeable sensations, that I resolved to prolong my stay on the water and, fixing the rudder in a direct position, stretched myself at the bottom of the boat. Clouds hid the moon, everything was obscure, and I heard only the sound of the boat, as its keel cut through the waves. The murmur lulled me, and in a short time I slept soundly.

Mary Shelley
from **Frankenstein**

Unit C. Assignment

Looking beyond style and plot (and yet we cannot totally ignore either one), we must see what the author has done to arouse and hold our interest.

> What verbs are used? Are they active, descriptive, or do they merely ascribe a state of being?

> Check the pronouns and the nouns which they refer to. Note any reference which is not perfectly clear.

> In any inverted sentences, do all expressions which precede the subject modify it?

> How does the author approach her readers through pronouns? Do the first-person references to the narrator give us an insight into his character? How?

> Keeping in mind the period in which **Frankenstein** was written (1818), do you feel you would have to reorder or reword any of the sentences to make them clear for the modern reader? If so, do so.

Module V

Unit D

What Makes Tone?

Tone is established by the writer's use of all the devices we have been discussing. One of the most often neglected devices is the use of the active voice in preference to the passive voice. The verb is usually acknowledged to be the tone-setting word in a passage. But the word in the subject position in a sentence is the one which centers the reader's attention. You are writing in the active voice when the **subject** of the sentence **does the action** of the verb. (I saw the dog swimming.)

When the **subject receives the action,** the sentence is in the passive voice. (The dog was seen to be swimming.)

Who did the observing? We don't know. If you decide that the dog is more important than the observer then by all means say "The dog was swimming."

On the whole, the active voice is more effective than the passive voice. From the reader's point of view the person who does the action is usually of greater interest than the object of the action. Consider these sentences:

Several students liked the course. (active voice; important word: "students")

The course was liked by several students. (passive voice; important word: "course" -- but the course is not doing the action, thus the whole idea is passive and bland)

In each case the subject assumes the importance. If, in fact, the course is more important than the students, it would be better to say:

The course appealed to several students. (active voice; important word: "course," and here the subject does the action -- a much more vigorous sentence)

Here we have a corrupted version of a passage from **Huckleberry Finn.** Naturally the original is in the active voice, past tense, which is conventional in novel writing. Here it has been transcribed, using the passive voice but maintaining the past tense.

·   ·   ·   ·   ·

As soon as we had been overtaken by night, the boat was shoved into the river. When she had been pushed out into the middle she was let go. She was allowed to float wherever she was pushed by the current. Then our pipes were lit, and our legs were dangled in the water. Nakedness was what was liked day and night, whenever it was permitted by the mosquitoes. My new clothes had been created by Buck's folks but proved to be too good to be comfortable. Besides clothes weren't really liked by me.

Sometimes the whole river would belong to us alone for the longest time. The banks and islands could be seen yonder, across the water; and maybe a spark was seen through a cabin window, and sometimes on the water a spark or two could be seen on a raft or a scow, you know; and maybe a fiddle or a song could be heard coming over from one of those crafts. Living on a raft appeared to be lovely. The sky was seen up there, all speckled with stars, and lying on our backs was what we did while the stars were examined, and whether they were made or just happened was discussed.

(based on Mark Twain)

Unit D. Assignment

You are going to be asked, now, to pat your head and rub your stomach -- as the kids do. Rewrite this passage in the **active voice** and **present tense**. You may have to change some of the words to get it to make sense. Hint: when you are confused about voice, ask yourself, "Who did the seeing, the hearing, or the pushing?" (Naturally, you will keep the past tense for "whether they were made or just happened.")

Module VI

Private Voice: Fiction

Module VI

Private Voice: Fiction

We may ask ourselves what makes a good story and think that an answer should come to us easily and quickly. Perhaps this is the answer that comes: a good story is one in which real people face real problems. But that much can be had through a long conversation with anyone who likes to complain out loud. That does not make a good story.

Maybe looking at it from the point of view of the reader may help us. As readers, what do we want? Why do we read? What are we hoping to find?

We seem to want one of two things: we want to be diverted and protected from life or else we want to be involved and drawn into life. Sometimes we want both simultaneously. The stories which divert usually offer us a view into strange corners which we have never explored. We meet odd amusing and attractive people we never met in real life.

But our more serious demands on fiction are those which can only be satisfied when we encounter characters who breathe with life, and ambiances and circumstances which we can acknowledge as similar to those we have always suspected exist. We do not find our relatives or neighbors or co-workers, but we do find characters who are provably human and predictably inconsistent -- just like real people.

And the problems? We want to see how other human beings are dealing with those basic insoluables which make up our own life. We know conflict, we know suffering. And (though most of us do not usually expose this knowledge) we know, too, what it is to have joy and fulfillment. But we each carry around bewilderments and private worries, ones we do not talk about or, in some cases, ones we talk about all the time. These are the subjects we want fiction to be concerned with.

The wise author knows that we are not interested in easy answers. We really do not want to be given solutions at all. We want to have the experience of seeing others dealing with the problems, and we want to see that they, too, are bewildered or fulfilled. And most of all, we do not want to have the problem or the solution explained to us. We want to do it ourselves.

Aristotle said of poetry (and by this he meant all imaginative writing): ". . . Poetry is something more scientific and serious than history, because poetry tends to give general truths while history gives particular facts."

That is in brief the essence of fiction -- that it should free us to conceive of the possibilities in existence. Fiction, like poetry, allows a writer to reveal to the reader an understanding of reality. We are moved by fiction which arouses in us a sensation of belief in what we read.

A writer is a person who knows a special way of

handling words so that ideas can be understood. True. But a writer is also a person who has something to say. That "something" may be defined as a glimpse of reality: what appears to be true and valuable. The willingness (desire, need) to communicate the glimpse of reality is what makes a creative person an artist. And a feeling for words is the quality of a writer.

We can say then that to test the workability of a story we must ask ourselves: "Do I believe that?" Facts and natural order are not the kind of believability I mean. Is the character true to what we know of human motivation and response? Is the interpersonal relationship valid? Is the human condition basically important to the characters involved? When the readers have experienced this vicarious existence do they have an increased understanding of life? The story need not be pompous and pretentious. It is the reader-response which should be great.

The elements of fiction are easy to list:

ambiance   - (time, place, atmosphere)
character   - (through action, reaction, speech)
situation   - (what happens? What causes it to happen? Often only enough is told to allow the reader to understand what could happen)
duration   - (usually begins at an established point in time and then progresses forward for only a short period)
conclusion - (handled by understatement)

Module VI

Unit A

Human Interest

The secret of what makes a good short story is not found in its elements, but in its handling. We are interested in the human condition, so human behavior is the stuff of which stories are made. A story has a theme -- a message -- but in the best stories the theme is felt, not read. The readers conclude what you are saying. They participate. You have not told them, you have shown them.

Unit A. Assignment

Look through the newspaper until you find an article which seems to have a human story hidden in it. Write the beginning of a story which reveals something about one person you feel may be involved in the situation. Hand in the clipping with your story.

Module VI

Unit B

Delineating Character

We reveal ourselves whenever we speak or move. We are revealed by what other people say and through what they do in relation to us. We show ourselves in action, or in inaction. And that is fortunate, for readers depend on revelation of character as their main avenue of understanding when they read a story.

You will have noticed that conversation is laid out in a special way in most stories. Tradition indicates that every time we change speakers in a story, we change to a new paragraph.

The stranger looked at me. "Do you live here?" he asked in a low voice.
"Yes."
"Well, there's something you should know."
I didn't really want him to go on.

You will notice that other words besides the quotation may be in a paragraph with the speaker's words. But the whole paragraph relates to the person speaking.

Thanks to this conventional arrangement, we can avoid using "he said" and "she said" over and over. The reader automatically knows that the speaker has changed when the new paragraph begins. Not all stories are written this way, but most are.

123

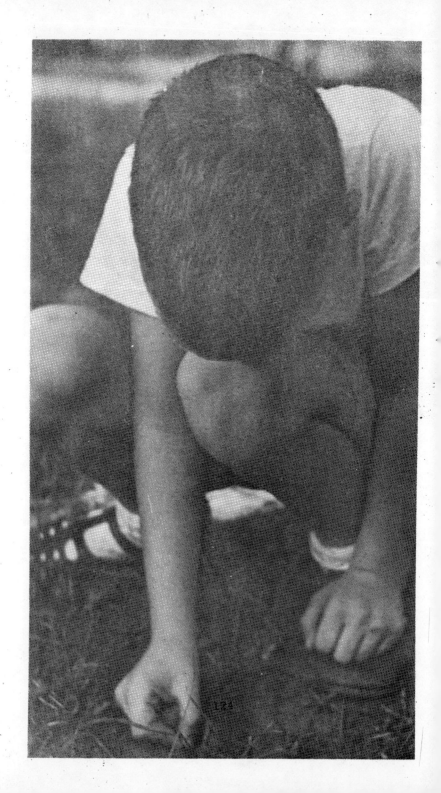

124

Unit B. Assignment

Look over the pictures which accompany this unit. Select a subject suggested to you by a person in one of the photographs. Remember, in a short story you will probably be able to reveal only one person well within the time and space limitation. Try to tell your story from the point of view of the main character. Tell only what that character could feel, think, see, hear, or know.

You will delineate this character by using some or all of the following:

>   dialogue
>   action
>   inner reaction
>   response to another character
>   interior monologue

Write a story (or the major portion of a story) which delineates this character.

Module VI

Unit C

Creating Ambiance

Webster says ambiance is "Environment; surroundings; especially, in painting and decorative art, the totality of supporting motives, patterns, or accessories surrounding and enhancing the central motive or subject of the design." In fiction you create ambiance for your characters when you establish the world in which the story's action takes place. Since you are limited in a short story by the very term "short," there should be NOTHING in the story which is not vital for the total effect.

This effect, this world created for your character has its physical aspect, its social condition, and its restrictions. These may be revealed by description, by dialogue, or by character action. All of these must be used to reveal, not to inform, to show and not to tell. Attached is another story which was written by a student in a class like this one. Notice what has been done to create a believable ambiance for the narrator.

HENERY AND ROMAND

Everyone was enjoying themselves that day. As I looked at Mrs. Smith, I began to think that she wasn't such a bad teacher, although I did not want her for my fifth-grade teacher. Before the party started, she told us that we had been her best fourth-grade class.

But the way she looked at Henery and Romand, it seemed as though she was saying to herself, "But, as for you two, I hope we never meet again."

Although it was the last day that thirty-eight kids would meet each morning from nine o'clock until three-thirty in the afternoon, this day would always be remembered by all thirty-eight. The last day was not only celebrated, but it was also the last day for revenge.

The closer it got to three-thirty, the friendlier Peggy, Mike, Joe, and many others got to Henery and Romand. Henery and Romand were the best fighters in the class. On the last day of school, the best fighters made a list of who they were going to beat up. And on the last day the scariest ones in class began to jump to do whatever Romand or Henery wanted.

About two-thirty, Peggy had already given Romand her ice cream and her cake. Mrs. Smith saw it and asked Peggy why. Peggy said she was getting full, but what Peggy was really getting was scared. Peggy managed to smile at Mrs. Smith as her eyes kept straight to see what time it was.

About ten minutes later, Mike came over and sat by Henery. Mike asked Henery did he want a bite of his hamburger. After Henery took the biggest bite he could, Mike said "I am full anyway, Henery. You can have it." Mike looked first to see if Mrs. Smith saw him, then he looked at Peggy and slowly looked over to see what time it was. Everybody in class knew what

Peggy and Mike were up to, and began to stop talking and dancing and sit quietly looking at each other in silence; racing to see who could smile at Henery and Romand as well as look at the clock before Mrs. Smith saw them.

About two-forty, Mrs. Smith said, "From the looks of Mr. Jones' class, they're having a good time. Does anybody in here dance?" Nobody said one word; just sat and ate quietly. Mrs. Smith put on a record and asked Joe to dance, but Joe said "No thank ya." Joe then immediately looked for Henery and Romand's approval. So, Mrs. Smith started dancing by herself. We wanted to laugh and start dancing but Henery and Romand gave the whole class that look that says "You bet not."

It was three o'clock now, and Mrs. Smith was handing out our report cards. After she finished, she told us to have a nice vacation and hoped that she would see us next year. Mrs. Smith walked to the back of the room and stood by the door as she usually does when class is out. Mrs. Smith said "Oh! Henry, Romand, would you two help me move the desks back? Thank you. The rest may go." Everybody looked startled, but glad, and ran out of the room like it was on fire. After about four blocks from school and looking back to see if Henery and Romand were coming, Peggy said "I sure do like Mrs. Smith." All thirty-six kids were all saying like an echo to Peggy; I do too; me too; and, I do too.

D. J.

Unit C. Assignment

Look again at the pictures attached to Unit B and select another character. Imagine a world for that character to live in (an acceptable ambiance) and a situation which reveals the conclusion you have come to most strongly about how such a person would respond to life. Keep yourself to this one idea. Use controlled language level, unified and simplified structure, and restricted subject matter to create a real character in a believable ambiance: in short, write a story (or major portion of a story) giving one strong unified impression.

Module VI

Unit D

Observing

The best advice a writer can get is: observe what is going on around you. Watch people. Make notes. Jot down what people say, what they do, how they get cornered by situations.

Do not worry about interpreting what you see. Let the characters demonstrate, through their words and actions, whatever truths there are to be noticed. Select habits and incidents to suit your needs, but be very observant about details, whether you use them or not. Tell your readers just enough to intrigue them, to draw them into the work, to awaken memories and feelings in them, and make them take part in the story. Remember that noticing odd, strange, interesting movements, gestures, clothing, habits can present a personality just as well as dialogue or action can.

Unit D. Assignment

Describe a person you have seen. (Select someone you do not know much about, but find interesting.) Tell about face and form, things worn and carried, posture and movement, and anything else that is out of the ordinary. Make this person very real for your readers. Do not explain or interpret. Leave that for your readers to do. Bring them into the story. Give them clues and let them draw their own conclusions.

132

Module VII

More Fiction

Module VII

More Fiction

The most aesthetically successful writer is the one who shows the readers how the characters feel, what they say (which is not always the same thing at all), and what they resort to doing. As readers, we hope to enter the story on a wave of sympathetic understanding. We are passive and non-intrusive, but we are feeling with the character as the experience presses in. We see that the protagonist is lonely as we have been lonely, or confused as we have been confused. We do not want to deal with little problems. Our involvement is with the enormous urges and frustrations of life: why doesn't anybody like me? What am I doing with my life? Which shall I decide: to compromise or to suffer the slings and arrows of outrageous fortune? But, because we are human and contrary, we do not want to read about great events and magnificent personages. Let us see the overwhelming question served up in a cereal bowl. The most soul-wrenching decisions have been reached in the most ordinary circumstances. The good short story material can be revealed in a store-window reflection, in the silence where there might have been a "hello." The small gestures which signal human vulnerability are the great moments in fiction.

And how will you get this message to us, to your readers? By showing and not by telling. When you tell us something, we view it suspiciously. "Why is the author saying this?" we wonder. Is the narrator (that

135

formless person whose voice recites the work) proving to be an unreliable narrator? Is he using this flat statement to deceive us? We trust our instincts better than we trust the voice which says, "This is so."

Let the readers come to their own decision about what is going on. Form a magical partnership: writer, character, reader. Let each one play a special part. The writer conceives; the character demonstrates; the reader interprets: that is an ideal arrangement.

Now even agreeing thus far, how are you going to go about writing a really good story? First, many of us believe, you must have in mind the general tone of the conflict you are going to write about. You may not be absolutely clear about the particular setting and characters, but you do know what trouble or irresolution you want to get yourself and your characters into.

The modern short story is no longer a tale, a narrative of situation and consequences which are strung out over long periods of time. The short story has one thing to reveal, and whatever that one thing may be, you have a short space of time to alert your readers to the power of the problem. The contemporary short story is like a small shuttered window in the blank wall of a dark room. Reader and writer stand side by side; the writer opens the window on a scene in action. Usually one person appears in clear view with a few others around him. Just as the reader feels that he would like to step through the window into the scene, the writer closes the shutters. The success of the story can be measured by the force of the impression which the reader carries away after the story ends.

You say, "That sounds easy; there must be more to it than that." Well, of course there is. Your characters, for example, must be real people. How do you create real people? First of all, you start noticing people. Why is Ruth not like Connie? Why are your uncle and your father so different? What does a three-year-old do that a five-year-old would never do? How does your co-worker speak at the end of the day compared to the way he spoke at the beginning? Why does everybody laugh at Charlie?

Then, you start recording everything you can remember about one person. Not how you felt about him, but what did he really do? Say? Wear? Carry? What are his mouth gestures? Hand gestures? Now comes the creative phase: what if that person were in a situation you noticed concerning someone quite different? How would he feel? If you know the answer to that last question, you will know what he would do.

Character and action: both must be true to life and yet must not be a mere recording of what actually happened. Instead of recording actuality (what happens every day), your story must deal with reality (what is true for all time). Much that is covered in the modules on poetry applies to the short story as well. When the writer has a strong sense that he has just been present at a moment when truth was revealed, that is the stimulus of creative writing.

What about style? You have recently come upon
Ronald Firbank or Robert Benchley and you have decided
at last you know the secret of success: it is style,
highly recognizable style. Well, yes and no.
Certainly no one who was charmed by William Saroyan
would mistake his prose for that of P. G. Wodehouse.
But a highly individualistic mode of writing is not
what any one of those writers depended on to establish
the reputation as a good writer. When you have turned
out a few volumes of stories you will find that you too
have a particular way of writing. The particular style
will have come to you as you write, as a result of
writing -- not as the cause of it. Write your stories
as they come to you. Learn by reading good writers,
all kinds of good writers. What there is about their
styles which appeals to you, you will unconsciously
(and unselfconsciously) draw into your way of writing.
You will be a blending of some qualities of all the
writers you admire. But the skeleton of your style
will be you, will be part of your way of thinking, way
of living, way of responding to life. Let your style
alone. Let it grow naturally. The best writing is
intuitive and the best style you can develop will be
the one which is the unaffected relfection of you.

Module VII

Unit A

Sensing a Situation

In your mind, go over the memories you have of occasions in which you witnessed conflict. These may be incidents in which you were involved or times when you were an observer. Remember, not all conflict is declared -- it may be present any time that a person works against another force, however mildly it is demonstrated. Human beings may be in conflict with nature, with society, with other people, or with themselves.

Attached is a story written by a student in this class a few years ago. Notice how successfully the author has revealed the essential conflict.

WILL

April third. The seasons all ran into each other so much these days that it was hard to notice when spring came.

He seated himself with his breakfast at the old oilcloth-covered table. It used to be grand to walk in the soft warm air. Emily always noticed the budding trees, the chirping birds, the new flowers. He could picture her with her soft blond hair, her blue eyes shining with pleasure over the bloom of the flowers.

139

He looked down at his coarse-skinned, gnarled hands, with the bunched blue veins tracking their way on the backs. A lot of things had changed.

His reverie was interrupted by shouts of laughter outdoors. Those rowdy children next door were at it again. He'd be lucky if his plants out front survived. The children next door would roller skate down the hill gathering momentum. And, unable to stop at the bottom, they would fall laughing and shrieking into his bushes. Just no concern for property.

He'd have thought they'd stop after gathering enough bruises and scratches to put most people in bed to heal. But, they would pick themselves up, sometimes with a few tears, and go at it again.

He hoped their parents were taking care of that house. It was the one he and Emily had lived in all the years of their marriage. She had taken such pride in her house and her yard. But, he could use the rent money these days, so he had moved into the little house next door.

His fingers tightened on the handle of his coffee cup as there were more shouts outdoors. Those kids again -- they couldn't do anything quietly. Will glanced out the window to see the older boy out there walking the fence while the rest yelled. Even the fence wouldn't last with that kind of use.

He sighed and shook his head. You'd think the parents would care about them breaking their reckless little necks. He looked over to the side of the other house. What was that child doing? She was digging in the flower bed Emily had been so proud of.

Will marched out the door and over to her as fast as he could, his hands trembling.

"See here, you. Stop that digging!"

The little girl looked up, surprised and frightened, dropped her trowel, and ran crying to her kitchen door. As she ran, her mother came out. The young woman comforted her child as she explained: "Betsy bought some gladiola bulbs with her allowance and has been so excited about planting them. I didn't think it would hurt anything."

Will's proud old back slumped and he shuffled off toward his house, muttering, "I'm too old, I'm too old."

Carol Anderson

Unit A. Assignment

List at least five occasions which you can recall taking part in a conflict or witnessing one. Select the one which appeals most strongly to you.

Now decide on your audience and consider what you have learned in Module I about reaching a particular audience.

You will have a message about conflict (that it is

within a person's very nature, that it is futile, that it ruins people, that it is the only way one can develop -- or some other conclusion). In the story itself, do not state your theme, but use the incident you remember to illustrate this theme. Do not feel restricted to using the facts as they happened -- remember Aristotle's words and tell what could have happened.

Write a story (or the major portion of a story) which shows conflict. Include an introductory statement (not part of the story) in which you summarize the effect you are going to create. Designate the audience your story is written for.

Module VII

Unit B

What if . . . ?

Writers generally do not retell events as they actually happened. They do not show people they know doing things that these people have actually done. Instead, writers observe. They notice how people behave; they become aware of motives and reactions, of folly and heroism. They tend to start dealing with observations of people and situations and then mix them together. "What if," they ask themselves, "that person over there were put into the situation I noticed yesterday?"

A good writer knows all about his characters. They have real backgrounds, identifiable ways of thinking, feeling, reacting. They went to school somewhere, voted some way, found husbands or wives, please them or annoy them. These facts may never surface in the story, but the author knows all about each character.

Unit B. Assignment

Someone in a story you are writing wants to tell about a place where he has been in the past. This character may be based on someone you observed somewhere -- but what if he talked about some place quite different? Write a description of this place in the voice of this fictional character. Be imaginative about both the place and the person speaking.

143

Module VII

Unit C

Says Who?

Why is a writer's work more interesting than a tape recording of the event being revealed in a story? The answer lies in the skill of the writer, in the creative ability to rid the scene of extraneous and tangential elements. The sensitive author has a way of emphasizing what is important and arousing the reader by understatement, implication, and suggestion.

Good material for fiction is all around us. As writers, we must spot characters who are going to get us started, who are going to remind us of what we want to demonstrate about the human condition. We must listen, too, to human dialogue. Often a comment overheard will be just what we need to remind us of things we have to say.

Unit C. Assignment

Go to a public place where you can observe people very different from you. Listen to what is being said. Use one exchange (one person says something and another answers) -- then you create the rest of the dialogue. Reveal the characters of the two people through this dialogue.

144

Module VII

Unit D

The Narrator

The main area still to be investigated in fiction is point of view: through whose eyes does the reader see the circumstances of the story? Whose voice is narrating?

Of all the stances a narrator may take in telling a story, there are four primary points of view:

1. **the narrating protagonist** (the main character presents his point of view in first-person narration). The "I" in this story is NOT the author, but is a fully created character.

    Such a story might begin, "I came into the room and stood close to the wall by the open doorway. The music was loud, too loud for such a small room. I wanted to leave, but I forced myself to stay."

2. **an observing character** (he is involved in the situation but only as a bystander)

    "While the party gathered in the over-furnished livingroom, Marcus kept watching the entrance. Suddenly, without sound or motion, a man appeared by the doorway, a man of no importance who made no impression on the noisy party."

145

3. **the omniscient author** (you will know everything going on, the thoughts and emotions of all the characters, or of most of them)

"The party was given late one night in May while Harvey was still planning to run for office. Aware of the importance of VIP's, Harvey had been afraid of overlooking anyone in town. The lone stranger who came uninvited never supposed that he would be noticed in such a crowd."

4. **the detached reporter** (this approach requires that you present only the FACTS which a reporter would know, and prohibits your knowing anything about the thoughts and emotions of any of the characters)

"It was May before a gathering was arranged. Everyone in town had been invited to the party at Harvey's beach house. Marcus was there, of course. And late in the evening a stranger appeared suddenly, a tall man who stopped in the doorway and looked around him."

Unit D. Assignment

Select one of these four points of view and limit yourself to that approach. Write a story (or the major portion of a story) based on someone or some event you remember from your childhood. Indicate which approach you have selected.

Module VIII

Private Voice: Poetry

Module VIII

Private Voice: Poetry

You are about to become a poet. It does not matter
whether you have ever written poetry before; a poetic
experience is available to everyone.

The satisfaction which comes from writing a poem is
a special kind of feeling. It is that underlying
reward found in creative experience, a very human sense
of accomplishment, available to most people. This is
not to say that anyone can write "Spelt from Sibyl's
Leaves" or "Under Milkwood" -- but almost anyone can
taste that sense of accomplishment known to Hopkins and
Thomas, Keats and Donne. True, it is as hard for a
minor poet to write a minor poem as it is for a major
poet to write a major poem. But there is the same
sense of basic satisfaction too. And that is worth
making a try for.

Before a ballerina moves to center stage, she has
become skilled in the fundamentals of ballet. Before a
Chichester up-anchors and turns tiller, he has
experienced wind and water, rope and canvas. The same
must be true for you as a poet. You must face facts
about poetry, its possibilities and restrictions. The
way you discover them is by learning from poetry which
you like. The way you test these out is to use them.

THE CREATIVE EXPERIENCE

There is almost no one who has not felt the urge to

149

be creative. Baking a cake, rebuilding a sports car, having a baby, writing a peace treaty, laying out an ad, folding paper into a swan -- these are all acts of creativity. In fact, every day we do many things which fulfill the basic requirements of creativity. There are five general areas through which a creative person passes: preparation, response to stimulus, incubation, experience of an epiphany, and ordering. Each is important and each must be experienced. They are parts of the whole.

PREPARATION: We are all training, all preparing, all learning constantly. As a poet you must learn that everything you do becomes a part of the future. Your very response to life is a kind of preparation of poems still to come.

Now learn to be perceptive. Your senses will be working for you, not merely to protect and inform you, but to refresh and excite you. Simple sense reactions, complex inner relationships, all are stored away in the possibility that you may want to recollect them in moments of tranquility. We all do this. Poets are blessed with an efficient system of recall -- or they have trained themselves to develop the skill over the years.

They also make associations. The inclination toward innovation (often mistaken for the creative process itself) is indulged in by the poet. You will not be afraid of synaesthesia, nor of a blending of sensuous response.

You are now going to respond through life situations. The commonplace will become extraordinary because you are never again going to be complacent. You will no longer expect each event, each interpersonal relationship, to fit a pattern. Each experience is a new event for you now.

You will not only be a person who experiences, but a person who responds to experiences. You will face your responses squarely; you will react, uninhibited. Later, you will recall your reaction, and reproduce -- synthesize -- that reaction, during a period of recollection.

You will learn to remember an emotion, an intuitive response, and learn to control that memory: to fragment it, to expand it, as a prism can break up and enrich a ray of light, as a chord can be augmented and diminished. Time is under control for the poet. You can expand or contract it, linger or delete as you see fit. Your fingers will hover over the controls, as it were. "Instant replay" and "fast forward" are among your decisions.

As you respond to your sense perceptions, the situation you find yourself in, the people you touch, your emotional reactions, so too you will react to ideas -- admitting, considering, reversing, inverting, trying out each idea for its creative potential.

A close study of the poetry which appeals most to you as a poet -- that is, in another poet's poetry -- will reassure you that sound as well as meaning contribute to your pleasure. And the most efficacious exercise the learning poet may indulge in is the reading and rereading of poetry which speaks to you of reality. That kind of opening of the mind prepares you to function as a poet.

STIMULUS: The second stage of the creative act involves the poet reacting to a stimulus. Prior to this, during the period of preparation, your creative power has been dormant. Now suddenly something wakes you. What can it be?

Frankly, it can be any one of many things. If you are just at the initial point of being a poet, it may be an assignment. "Write a poem," you are told in a class of learning poets, and you are shocked, affronted, offended. But when you put pen to paper, you write. Sometimes, at this first try, it is a very good poem. More often it is a crack in the facade of prose, a tentative outpushing toward new form. But this is the first motion toward poetry.

What else do we know about the stimulus? We can isolate three qualities, three essentials to which it is related. First, immediacy. The experience to be revealed, whether physical, intellectual, or emotional, is one which presses on the poet's consciousness. Next, intensity. As a poet, you are stimulated by a force too importuning to be resisted. And lastly, reality. You have a stirring which relates to truth, to reality as you perceive it, and whether conscious, unconscious, or subconscious this stirring urges you to start doing something about what you feel.

The stimulus can be as common as an assignment, as amorphous as an inner stirring, as actual as a scene viewed or a sound heard. It can come as a vague disturbing memory. Its form is not important. But you learning poets must alert your senses to respond to whatever stimulus reaches you, must let the poem start to take form within you.

INCUBATION: For when you are reached, you react and in a way which is undefinable. We call this period "incubation" for want of a better word. The poem is in the process of becoming a poem. At this level no one can help the poet. And during this time very few can understand you.

Sometimes the period is brief -- no longer than it takes to catch the spirit of the thing and transfer a feeling or thought to word and phrase. Sometimes, though, it is almost interminable. This must be your problem. You may be jotting down word clusters and cadences. You may be sulking and preoccupied. You may, on the other hand, be playing especially good tennis or lecturing coherently. But in any case this period is sacrosanct; no teacher of learning poets has any business interfering during this time. Nor has anyone else. It is a time unknown and unmeasurable. As a poet, you can deny its existence, but you cannot escape it.

EPIPHANY: Suddenly the poem makes its appearance. Words take the place of intuitive non-verbal response which you were feeling.

153

Once in a while (as in the case of an in-class assignment) there will seem to be no time at all between the stimulus and the epiphany. Consequently you may feel that you have no need for incubation -- that you are special, an instant-poet. Occasionally you are right, or partially right. Not all poems result from long submerged incubation. Sometimes an idea seems to catch fire from the stimulating spark and a poem cries out to be recorded at once. Sometimes we do have that special experience -- a kind of **veni vini vici**. Actually though, in most cases, the incubation has been taking place in the dark, unnoticed, started by some other stimulus, long since forgotten. The two responses touch and run together ready for release -- and there you have it, the ready poem.

We know much about this moment when the poem declares itself. Poets like to talk about it because it gives a validity to that blank unfathomable period of incubation they have just survived. They write. They bring into existence the anticipated manifestation. Most poets write when they sense that the moment has come. They use shoe cartons, old envelopes, margins of books. If they are lucky, or provident, they go into an empty room and shut the door. Almost without exception they find pleasure in the act of recording the poem as it comes to them. This is the most rewarding moment of creativity.

With the arrival of the poem in a transmittable form comes that intense desire to have someone read the poem or hear it read aloud. Wise poets can resist this urging until after some sense of order has been imposed on the first rush of words. Most cannot resist.

The pleasure of the ephiphany blended with the dark sequence of incubation and the pending cold sobering peiod of intellectual ordering make up the whole reality of the experiencing of a poem. Pleasure and pain, intake and output, intuitive pouring forth and conscientious ordering: these are the dichotomies of creativity.

ORDERING: The intuitive response as poem is a triumph, and the poet who is pleased by this experience is behaving just as poets ought to behave. But unless you are a practicing poet (and not always then) you are not yet free of your responsibilities toward this poem. By a "practicing poet" we mean what is almost impossible to find: a poet who practices his art as a musician practices for a concert: long hours, much drudgery, enormous self-discipline. The poet, as we have earlier acknowledged, needs proficiency in several areas: in sensing reality, in involvement in word meaning and in dealing with cadence and sound. So remain intuitive in your awareness of reality, your sense of "message" (here, if at all, we may find evidence of the "natural" poet). But in other areas you must learn your skill and practice to improve it.

Module VIII

Unit A

Getting Started

Certain facts of life are inescapable. One is that as a learning poet you will write about yourself. Since this is natural and universal it seems to be a good beginning for you. A workable first assignment for you is to write about an immediate experience: something that happened to you today or yesterday. You are learning, among other things, that we all have moments of truth, moments when we sense reality, and that these revelations are not necessarily connected with the dramatic once-in-a-lifetime events.

Here is a student's poem as it appears in blocks of four stages of expression but set on the page in a pleasing pattern.

EMERGENCE OF NEW

Spiraling windward
    my emotions leave dust whirl
    of uncertainties
Sand mounds
    or levels of being
    cushion my step
Reactions of the other survivors
are muddied with past references.

Linda Ware Austin

156

Starting your career as a poet by writing a four-line poem seems valid: the poem is encompassing enough to allow you to make a single complete statement, yet limited enough that it is not terrifying.

Not all four-stage conceptions end up as four-line poems. Sometimes the opening of an idea requires an expanded line structure.

Unit A. Assignment

This first assignment is gauged to produce a poem of limited dimension. In being assigned a four-line poem you are being given a set of fences to restrict you, a small plot to cultivate. Meter and verse pattern are at your discretion.

Here is one pattern you may want to follow:

first line, statement of experience

second, your sense reaction -- any sense or combination of senses

third, your emotional reaction

fourth, your conclusion -- which you should try to express in an understatement. Since successful poetry must involve the reader in its conclusion, this use of understatement stresses the idea that the poet and the reader together give meaning to the poem.

157

An alternate pattern is for a four-liner which progresses thus:

    first line, vision: what you see
    second, position: how you are involved
    third, action: what you do
    fourth, reaction: how you feel

Now try your hand at poetry.

Write a few four-line poems. Do not worry about rhymes, do not try to make your poetry rock back and forth like a nursery rhyme or a song. Just use your own natural speech. Let the poetry flow as freely as it wants to.

Module VIII

Unit B

Creative Experience

Confidence in form will lead you to experimentation, but do not be surprised if all these early works are subjective. Poets talk about themselves; so do we all. But if you have an apt touch you will turn this poetic revelation into a universal statement. We will suffer with you, take joy with you, not so much because we are compassionate but because your experience calls forth an echo in us. We see ourselves. We see truth. You have admitted us to your glimpse of reality.

You will move slowly from a contemplation of your experience to an observation of life around you or life as you imagine it. You will tell not only of what you do but what all people do. You will still be involved, of course, but objective. You will become more musing and less emotional. Your highly subjective response is universalized. Now you are becoming something of a philosopher. Often you will resist telling the conclusion, only present the reader with observable facts. You will open the door of poetry and admit the reader as one of the major members of the cast.

Here are two poems written by former students. In each case, the student made a connection. In the first one the poet notices a similarity which stirs her emotions and seems to point out a pattern.

PRIVATE BLUE

Copenhagen on a bare canvas
Bachelor button yawning open
Bridal garter, satin trimmed
Woolly blanket, faded now
Wedgewood coloring a prized teapot
Crushing glare of a child beloved.

J. Guest

In this next poem, a poet notices a moment in nature and connects it with the past.

GREY BROWN BIRD

Grey brown bird
Plain and common,
Swallow? Sparrow?
A voice but no song,
On a branch--
In a cat's catch.

Reminder
Of a grey brown childhood,
And a girl who would rush
To defend you.

J. Bidart

As your experience with poetry expands, you will find yourself relating one event to another, one intimation to a quite different area of thinking.

Poetry is supposed to do this to you. Any time you notice a stirring of feeling, an echo of truth sounding in what you are experiencing and observing, be glad. That is poetry getting ready to be written down.

Unit B. Assignment

Write a few poems, now, based on the most usual source material for poetry:

> Think about an experience you have had which seems to you to be significant. It need not be an earth-shaking event; sometimes the small acts and minor tremors are signs to us that something meaningful has taken place. Keep free as you write. Let the words flow.

> You notice people. You watch what is happening around you. But maybe you are not yet in the habit of transferring your observations to concise, succinct poems. If you do not know how to begin, list all the nouns that relate to this moment of observation. Now find vital forceful verbs to bring life to them. Keep your language simple but your words alive. Do not say one word more than you need to say.

> Set up an equation. Relate today to yesterday or tomorrow; show the difference between here and there. Describe the inside of something which other people only know the outside of. Isolate yourself from the group, or merge with the flow of nature. Show order out of chaos.

161

Module VIII

Unit C

Cadence

One of the most important ingredients of poetry is cadence, the rhythmic quality of speech which gives lyric poetry that special appeal to the ear. Since cadence and movement are closely related, what more fitting subject matter than imitative motion in poetry. You can say through the form of your poem just what you say through word-meaning. This is decorum: that the poem should show motion while it tells about it. Use of typography -- spacing of the poem on the page --here is another poetic device to experiment with. Progression and sequence of idea depict motion. Special sounds, isolated or in combination, add to the feeling. Meter and rhythmic cadence control the reader's response.

If we decide to write a poem about motion we are going to imitate that motion in the form of our verse. Certain devices help convey the idea of motion.

First, the run-on line. When poets gave up the restrictive form of conventional verse, about the turn of this century, they claimed the right to determine independently just where each line should end. We say today, just this many words and sounds and ideas will go on the line, then the reader will have a brief flick of time before he starts on the next line. We control the reader by controlling the line break.

162

Here is a poem about dancing which, in itself, has
a strong sense of motion.

ONCE MORE AROUND

When the wheat is just out,
The earliest blossoms
Are still pushing buds,
The hummingbirds not back,
And just a few toads are about;
Before the sun gets high
And the bees' wings dry,
I sneak off, without my shoes,
For a roving, rambling walk.

As if my bare soles
Were not enough contact
With earth, I take in hand
A straight stick off the ground
-- Later trading it for a crooked one --
And drag it along behind.

Wandering, I seek a patch
Where the grass is already tall
And the dew is settled heavy.
There, in hopping-jumping-twirling steps,

I dance the rite of cycles,
Baptizing my feet anew,
To go once more around.

                    J. Bidart

Here is a poem about someone driving by (among other things).

RETIRED

I thought I saw you pass
        my house
the other morning
driving a big blue car
        you never owned
smoking a pipe
        the way you do
and looking splendid.

It wasn't you.
You didn't look my way
        or wave
        or raise your pipe
the way you do.
It wasn't really you
        looking salaried
        and late for work
and splendid.

Anne Passel

The first line might have been, "I thought I saw you pass my house the other morning." The thought is intentionally broken into three pieces because that gives a clearer picture of passing by. Such small devices as line break can control the reader through a run-on line. A pause in the middle of the line also controls motion. A line with an end-stop stops motion:

        "and looking splendid."
Repetition either of syntactic pattern or of idea gives
a feeling of motion. So the case of this poem,
        "You didn't look my way
            or wave
            or raise your pipe"
attempts to include the futility and familiarity of the
repeated gestures.

    The repetition of words and ideas here contrasts
illusion with actuality but gives a sense of
continuance or motion too. The repeated "the way you
do" relates to the man's habit of smoking a pipe. "It
wasn't you" becomes "It wasn't really you." And the
hopeful image "and looking splendid" is cut down to
actuality in "It wasn't really you / looking . . .
splendid."

            Unit C. Assignment

    Try your hand at a poem of motion -- even two or
three of them. Use any of the devices discussed above
and whatever else makes the poem full of motion.

Module VIII

Unit D

Image and Metaphor

First, let's clarify our terms.

"Image" means merely a picture, a word picture which creates a vivid impression on your reader.

"Metaphor" is a little more complicated, but metaphor is the primary device used in poetry. By definition it is "an implied analogy which imaginatively identifies one object with another and ascribes the qualities of the first one to the second." A simpler way of looking at a metaphor is this: it presents something unknown to the readers in terms of something they know. Wordsworth refers to the evening as being "quiet as a nun." You didn't know about that particular evening; you do know about nuns. His relating them metaphorically has told you clearly about what was unknown to you.

Sometimes we do not say "as" or "like," merely give the unknown the attributes of something the readers know about. "The Soul selects her own Society," Emily Dickinson tells us, "Then shuts the Door." The metaphor reminds us of how it feels to be closed out. Now we know something new about this particular soul.

The learning poet who experiments with imagery is enjoying the full pleasure of writing poetry. Imagery is the use of visual reference; yes, and it is a skillful handling of figures of speech, and the interrelationship of these devices with the poet's basic thesis. But it is more besides. Images are the outward and visible signs of the interior meaning of a poem. Images create the ambiance in which ideas prosper.

Imagery succeeds in poems when you become poet in the truest sense of the word: not only because you are a person who has thoughts and feelings which grow into poetic utterances but because the very shape of your thoughts moves the reader to say, "There. That's right. That's just how I feel. Now I know: that's how it really is."

This picture of the cemetery at St. Philip's Church in Charleston, South Carolina, establishes a mood. But notice in the accompanying poems how the poets have given different responses to the idea of death.

DEATH DIES

Death dies in the piney prison.
Shut away from the very air,
By shroud and soil smother-sheltered.
Decay denied, release is caged.

Unbox the body and lay it out
As a feast for hungry Hertha.
To her who has nourished the flesh,
Give back what is owed.
J. Bidart

I HEARD NO CRYING

I heard no crying on the sleeping hillside
Only with winterbright sun and dancing breeze
When we buried Grandpa Oxley.
Even as the sons and daughters of sons and
                                    daughters of
Sons and daughters ringed the fresh cut grave
I heard no crying on the mountain.

The young men grandsons -- many more than six --
carried and followed the coffin while we sang:
"Will the circle be unbroken?"
And oh how new the sun fell on the still grass
How quiet the wind rhythmically slipped
                                    with our breath!
But we did not cry in the December morning.

Grandpa, we did not grieve aloud
In the soft sun of distant spring.
We gathered arm in arm remembering
The tree by waters with fruit in its season.
We linked immortal to your name
and blessed the fullness of your years.

                                    Catherine Crown

Unit D. Assignment

Look at something in nature -- anything you choose
connected with water, air, or earth. However involved
we are with city living, we are basically related to
the natural flow of life and we respond to the

essential forces of nature. Allow the impressions you received to stimulate you to respond. Let your imagination run free. Now write as many poems as you want to have criticized, and include the following:

an image related to sound
an image related to color
an image related to motion
an extended metaphor (one metaphor carried throughout the poem)

Indicate in the margin of your paper whenever you have used one of these devices.

Module IX

More Poetry

172

Module IX

More Poetry

Before we talk further about writing, let us consider your response to poetry. You must face the fact, first of all, that poetry is eminently a communication and like any message it involves the speaker's attitude toward his audience and his attitude toward his material.

The listener who hears your poetic message may be the world at large, those who (from your point of view) need conversion, a sympathetic coterie, a particular individual, or maybe merely your other self. Whether you are addressing the one or the many, you must feel this urgency to communicate and must relax your social being (disciplined, repressed) long enough to write down the insistent urgings which clamor to be spoken. That is all. If your inner voice speaks unrepressed it will use the proper tone.

And what will it speak of? Of the poet's major concerns, surely. Poetic subject matter is as varied as the world of fact and the world of idea. As long as you feel moved to convert, convince, expose, reveal, share, you will be dealing with poetic matter. It is how this revelation is expressed that makes poetry.

Because all poetry has these six attributes, these six testables: an expression of reality, an integral unity, abstraction into imagery, selection of the exact word, an underlying cadence, and sense of sound.

1. Reality -- the moment of truth -- is not to be confused with actuality, which is merely the everyday happening of life. Reality differs for each one of us, but when you know suddenly, intuitively, undeniably, that you have had a glimpse of what is true and right and special, that is your moment of contact with reality. As a poet, you know that you must share this experience: that is the function of poetry, the destiny of the poet.

2. Organic unity has been defined as that sense of wholeness which leaves out nothing that is essential and includes nothing that should be omitted. Every poem which is successful in its basic purpose will prove this definition. Each word and image add to the primary force to be experienced when one hears the poem. The full experiencing of the poem is the vicarious awakening to the reality known to the poet.

3. Imagery is more than pictorial expression: it is the device by which you transfer the vision you have had of reality into a mode of expression acceptable to the reader, the uninitiated, the receiving mind. Imagery is not merely the turned phrase, the charming word cluster: it is the very essence of poetry. It is the simple equation which states that this Known and that Known when combined together and viewed inside-out equal the ponderable Unknown. Image and metaphor, symbol and allusion, all serve to pin-prick your readers into participating in the act of the poem. The closed mind cannot receive poetry. When readers stir

174

their own recall, waken to echoes and harmonics, that is the moment when poetry has succeeded. Poetry must be not only vocal but evocative. It must cause the readers' mind to speak to them. And for this reason it cannot speak of actuality, which is only tolerable, but of reality, which is vital. And for this same reason it must speak in a reader-involving idiom: the response-invoking algebra of imagery.

4. The Imagists of the 1920's included in their dictum what poets have always known about poetry, that true poetic language involves using the "right word." How could it be put more simply? As the basic dimension of poetry depends on distillation and condensation we must not be surprised to find that minimal length also involves exactness. You know hundreds of words. You use only a special few. Your skill as a craftsman rests on a highly developed sense of selectivity. Emily Dickinson left us a clue as to the complexity of the problem of selection. In forming the symbolic combination of words which would rouse the reader to recapture the idea in her mind, she listed her choice of words; in writing "the Bible is an antique Volume" this poet ultimately chose: "Had but the Tale a thrilling Teller." She made an early choice and a later emendation, but before her initial selection of "thrilling" she tried out and rejected the following words: typic - hearty - bonnie - breathless - spacious - tropic - warbling - ardent - friendly - magic - pungent - warbling [sic] - winning - mellow.[1]   Every poet recognizes this

maze, this bewildering decision which must be made among alternatives. The road not taken is as inviting as any other. But for each poem, each fragment, only one decision will be the one which matters. A manuscript with deletions and substitutions might be the definition of a poem.

Sometimes there is no need for the exhausting revision, the word search, the trying-out of phrases. It is a blessed poem indeed that spills forth in its perfected form. It is a rare one, though, rare for the master craftsman or neophyte. And somehow suspect. Often intimacy with the experience, with the immediacy of poetic reaction, may make you overly respectful of your first fresh outpouring. A little space of time, a little objective distance will allow you to see that intellect as well as intuition functions in poetry writing.

5. Poetry is the contemporary descendant of the oral-formulaic family of song. Basically poetry is song. Its appeal is through the ear to the mind or heart or spirit -- wherever it is going. Primitive cultures speak in cadenced structure; children love verse, love rhythm and pattern. Response to poetry is intuitive, irresistible for most of us.

Basic rhythmic repetition is one of the identifiable elements of verse. Children learn lists of facts by setting them to song pattern. "Thirty days hath September" we recall, "Here I come. Where from? New orLEENS." We depend on "I

before E, except after C" and "First Washington,
Adams, Jefferson; James Madison, James Monroe."

Modern poetry has broken free from the intensity of
stress in what one student (unconsciously wise)
referred to as "didactic pentameter." But the
cadence which serves as the armature for
contemporary poetry is not less dependable for
being less discernible. What was formerly the
metre and foot of poetry has been replaced by
tension and balance in the poetics of today.

Cadence: what can we call it? "A rhythmic
sequence or flow of sounds in language," Webster
tells us. We are really dealing with counterpoint
in modern poetry; with a kind of speech-cadence
tautly counterbalanced by thought-cadence. Syntax,
even rearranged syntax, imposes a rhythm on speech.
Thoughts, even fragmented thoughts, result from a
natural process. The pattern may be as subtle as
the echoes and harmonics of association or as
hooked-together and interrelated as logical
sequence. But both result in a patterned cadence.
A perceptive examination of any successful modern
poem will reveal other counter-stressing cadences.
Imagistic patterns, metaphoric extensions,
allusionary inner echoes all set up their own
tensions, their own cadences. But for the learning
poet it is enough, at first, to become aware of the
patterns of speech working in counteraction to the
balancing of ideas and thoughts; a woof and a warp,
straining one against and with the other, to create
the full fabric of poetry.

177

6. An ear for sound is basic equipment for the poet. As end-rhyme has lost its hold as the be-all and end-all of the poetic line, other uses of sound have been established. A clue for the composition of poetry which sings with the element of beautiful sound is this: echo. The poem which echoes the stressed vowel sound of its key word insists meaning and sound simultaneously. Alliteration is almost unavoidable, and the use of the triplet, that thrice-run bell, seems almost instinctive for the learning poet. But alliteration had its hey-day in Anglo-Saxon times and has been the easy out for poets ever since.

Instead, the subtle interweaving of echoes and intonation of vowel sounds (assonance) while familiar to poets of all time, has become the mark of the twentieth-century poet. The use of internal rhyme becomes a natural associate of the echoed vowel sound. The learning poet will do well to demand that le mot juste be juste in sound as well as meaning.

[1]The Poems of Emily Dickinson, edited by Thomas H. Johnson, (Cambridge, Mass.: The Belknap Press of Harvard University, 1955), p. 1067.

Module IX

Unit A

Sound

Learning poets should learn one basic fact about sound, that the most successful poem is a resonant and integrated sound pattern. Stressed words throughout the poem interweave a pattern, complex or simplified, which insists a repetition of vowel sounds wherever such a repetition reinforces meaning. No inharmonious vowel sound is isolated in a company of integrated sounds.

Look at a poem, almost any good poem. When you read it aloud it sounds great, but to the uninitiated it is based on magic. Under careful examination, we can see that the poet has created a complex sound pattern and has caught us up in wonderful echoing of repetitions.

Let us go through this student poem and circle all the words which are major words -- important in meaning and also placed in the poem where a stress comes in natural speech rhythm.

Note the series of columns on the right, one for each vowel. In each column, you will find the vowel sound which appears in the major word in that line. If you check, you will see that all of the dominant vowel sounds are echoed somewhere in the poem.

Nowhere

I trace a pattern of loneliness
entwining curving paths
which lead nowhere
Each slender line begins with a
flourish
but ends in paling trailings
Indistinct
Undefined

A	E	I	O	U
ā̆a			ō	
a	ɚ	ī		
			ō	
	e	ī̆i		
	ɚ			
āā	e			
		ĭ		
		ī̄		

J. Guest

When you do this to your own poem, realize that you
are giving a sound check to your work which many people
know little about. Take advantage of your findings.
Your sounds may not echo as clearly as the sounds do in
"Nowhere." When you find orphans (no relatives
anywhere in the poem) don't hesitate to substitute
words with more harmonious sounds. Sometimes you may
come across just one word with no echo. Maybe it is
isolated intentionally (or intuitively) to call special
attention to that word. Such attention has negative
overtones; the sound will jar the readers, upset them,
disturb them. If that is what you intended, great. If
not, you know what to do.

Unit A. Assignment

Select a poem you have written (preferably one new
for this occasion) and let us experiment in sound.

Circle the key words in your poem. They must be in

180

the right position to be stressed when the poem is read aloud.

Now sound aloud the vowels in these key words. These will be the major vowel sounds in your poem. (Mark them in columns as we did for "Nowhere.")

Adjust the sound so that all major sounds have echoes. Substitute new words for those which have sounds not related to any other major word in the poem.

When you hand in this assignment, include all the versions of your poem.

Module IX

Unit B

Form

Sometimes the form of the poem on the page tells us almost as much as the words do. Length of line influences the readers; they sense the implication of brevity, the complexity of extention.

AFTER

After
Hard words
Bare harsh feelings
In quaking pride-quickened voice,
Wavering discontent wins, distance beckons,
And the heart quavers in facing final division--
Healing rites undertaken with a gentler look,
Promise in a hand offered to touch,
Anxious, soft-toned phrases,
End in love, relieved,
Affirmed.

                                        J. Bidart

Applying the discipline of form to the profusion of thought becomes both irresistible and desirable for the poet. What fascinates us about chess can astound us in poetry. Every poet should let himself be tempted into experimentation with form. To invent a form is an achievement. Further, to accept the preconceived form has its own rewards: to write a sonnet, a successfully achieved sonnet, is to ally oneself with a host of poets over the ages. Restriction and limitation on the surface lead to exploration of depth and height. But beyond the level of challenges there is more to intrigue us about the intricacies of form. Verse pattern is a further expansion and involvement with pattern in general. It is a ramification of the sequence and overlapping of ideas, the tension of cadence, the echo of sound. It is the very essence of poetry.

Sometimes space can give the illusion of isolation. Position of lines on a page can show people together or a person alone. In the following poem, "Brief Encounter," notice that the words spoken fit exactly into the space between the people. See, though, how separated they are at the end.

BRIEF ENCOUNTER

"Hello"
I said   to you
        and the
        word
took shape, tone, form
expanded and became
    took our hands
    ran with us
    laughed
down wind   down hill
waltzing turns, leap landings
vortex, whirlwind, and eddy
    "What?"
then I looked   across at you
        and emptiness
        stretched between us
        "Goodbye"
I said   to you
        and the word
    put its hands in its pockets
scuffed its feet   shrugged off
                and you
        put your hands in your pockets
                and turned away
            to listen to someone else
and I
put my hands in my pockets
and I squeezed my palms
and I could feel the crumbs and lint
in the pocket seams and in the day.

Anne Passel

Unit B. Assignment

Look at these two poems, paying special attention to the form the poets have used. Now try some experimentation. Write some poems following the instructions below:

> Write a patterned poem in which the form of the written poem on the page gives a clue about the content: short lines indicate beginning or completion, simple idea, or direct approach; long lines show complexity or involvement, or something which takes a long time in happening.
>
> Invent a pattern; use line length, rhyme repetition, stanza form -- whatever you like. Include a brief explanation of your pattern.

Module IX

Unit C

Allusion and Symbol

Poetry moves successfully from the tangible sensuous world into the abstract world of idea. The poet who involves the readers' minds and spirits along with emotions and memories is fulfilling that poetic requirement that the reader and poet are partners in bringing the poem to life. Poets are people whose words mean more than they say. Poets use readers' minds and memories, all they have read and thought: what myth suggests and reveals, the overtone and echo which a word evokes, the ambiance and connotation which lurk in a symbol.

There are three kinds of symbols which writers use, often without knowing one from the other. The most easily recognized symbol is the universal symbol, evocative and moving, which appeals to many people in many different cultures. Fire is such a symbol. The snake, the tree, the sea are meaningful to many peoples. The next most familiar symbol is the local symbol, words and references which have special significance in the particular era. You will be able to think of many of these.

Most specialized is the poet's symbol, special for one person and often consistent throughout one poet's work. The following poem uses all three kinds of symbols.

DESTINATION

The well-tended green rolled on forever.
Granite slabs interrupted abruptly
                      the speckled acre.
Nostril lining damp with heavy air
Slightly obstructing freedom.

The deadened stillness reached up
And gently eased my skirt.
My coat was hanger-clad hooked to the Yew.
The suit coffer was opened and waiting.

I folded up neatly
And packed myself in.

                                J. Guest

The "well-tended green," "granite slabs," and "Yew"
present a cemetery which is universal in implication.

The reference to a "coat . . . hanger-clad" says
something clearly about our own time and place. And
the idea of folding up "neatly" to conform to death is
a symbol which belongs to this poet alone.

When you use an allusion (a reference to literature
or history) you are depending on your readers to bring
their prior knowledge to the poem. You are counting on
overtone and echo to enrich the reading experience.
You allude to a reference you share with your readers
-- but you merely allude, you do not explain what you
are doing.

You may have noticed various allusions in the student poems included in the modules. In the next poems you write, embed an allusion or two: familiar expressions from poetry or drama, a name or reference from literature or history.

THE DRAGON ROLE

Beneath the horse's belly
    - white, bulging, wet with sweat -
the dragon humps himself
bearing, yet fearing the hooves
        bunched muscle-thrust
        against the brittle plates
        the scalloped overlapping
wing huddled close
claws dug to the quick in the earth
contorted neck
wild eye rolling fearsomely
        to see the foot in mail
        brass leggings to the knees
        thrust over the horse's heaving side.
His dragon gorge rises in fire
hot fumes, dry breath-heat
        the belch of it
        presses against his throat
he twists again, one life-wrung undulation
        avoiding and dreading
        the sharp deflating
        terminal incision.

Yet who is to say that this is not the first
the only specimen sword-proof and lance-immune
the single dragon destined to survive
exultant and triumphant?

So, since this may be so,
in case through him
the dragon role converts
the dragon hero lives:
he suddenly yawns-open jaws and jowls
and with the spewing forth of fire and fumes
waits - and will he receive the burnished pike
along the hollow grooving of his tongue?

                                Anne Passel

The picture of St. George brought about this poem. Notice, though, that you do not have to have the traditional response to familiar legends and myths. The attitude of the dragon became more interesting than that of St. George. Actually the poem is really about a young idealist instructor who seemed to be trying to be a hero at a time when the lethal spear was just ready to pierce him to the quick.

Unit C. Assignment

Try your hand at allusion and symbol.

Write a poem which is subtle in its use of allusion. Call forth a feeling by reminding the reader what another poem or novelist has introduced in some other work. (When T. S. Eliot has Prufrock say, "No I am not Prince Hamlet," he knows that you know what Hamlet is all about. He has borrowed Shakespeare's symbol to furnish you with a short-cut into Prufrock's character.)

See if you can use all three kinds of symbols, not necessarily all in one poem. Write as many poems as you like.

Ordering

Let us acknowledge that the poet is the wielder of words who willingly accepts the basic premise of restriction and limitation. A poem is unified, it is reduced to the essentials, it may even hold itself within the limits of preconceived pattern. The writer who is poet -- not essayist nor treatist nor author of a twenty-volume series -- this poet then has agreed to brevity and condensation, in fact sometimes almost distillation.

You will do well to be flexible in rewriting. A new version of the same poetic conception will often startle and delight its creator. Sometimes expansion of an idea (but more often a contraction of it) will seem to awaken you to a more pertinent self-expression.

All poets experiment with turn of phrase: the rearrangement of syntax, the act of verbing it with nouns or nouning it with verbs, the omission of redundancies, the substitution of feeling for being or being for seeing. All these moving of ideas through words are part of the poet's exercise in ordering.

As essential as meaning is sound in poetry. The final word choice in a poem must reflect both considerations. Naturally there will be compromise. But whatever experimentations afford best results in blending exact meaning with salubrious sound, these are the experiments which you must go through.

Intuitive poetic response, then, tempered by an understanding of the possibilities of form in verse, will bring about the act of ordering poetry. You know for whom you are writing. This knowledge both results from and influences your selection of language. You know your readers as you know your material. They must be considered while you are imposing order on your poems.

Unfortunately you will become aware of your critics too. A wounding experience in the past may make you over-cautious or inhibited. This is one area in which an instructor can help the poet. A zealous guardianship of the poetic ego is essential to the care and feeding of poets. Later, when this proprietary parenthood has been relaxed a little, when the new poem is permitted a life of its own, then an instructor may want to be more analytic and critical. But during the creative process, even at this late stage in the process, we remember that you poets are vulnerable indeed.

When you have ordered your verse and are satisfied that it reveals what you intended to reveal, you will probably breathe a sigh of relief and turn away from the poem to something quite different. Your problem is now to become non-protective toward your work. This objectivity is not easily achieved. The passage of time frees the poet, though, and you will sooner or later be able to view your poetry as less than an integral part of yourself.

Once this stage is reached, the poem has become a
communication -- which was, after all, what it was
intended for. Now you reread it. Maybe you can sense
further need for ordering, a need which can fortunately
be postponed until the propitious moment for revision.
But perhaps you like it. Perhaps now, wonderfully, it
conveys that view you had of reality, and conveys it in
a way which is succinct and exact, nicely turned in
phrase and beautifully musical. Now you are a poet.

It is hard to talk about revising a poem. The poet
does not think of it as merely cosmetic surgery; it is
a serious and deeply considered act. As you revise,
you will know what has to be done.

This next poem began as a reaction to a couple who
visited us one weekend. They treated each other in a
way which was disturbing to see. They seemed like
parakeets. The first version of this poem is a simple
description of the couple.

In the revised version of the poem, the bird image
emerges as the strongest part of the poem. The final
version talks directly about parakeets, with the
metaphor relating them to people as a kind of reversal
of the original metaphor. The readers are then called
upon to make their own connection to the general
comment about human beings.

You will notice that the revising is not only in
terms of the metaphor, but that the basic sound of "er"

(as in "her") has been emphasized. To this sound has been added the aggressive long "I" sound (as in "my"), "Partly turned aside / firm on the perch. . . ." You may catch other patterns if you read the poem aloud.

(First Version)

She is silent when he speaks
she is not listening
thinking merely
brooding
imagining an answer.

And when he stops
when he turns to her
there is a flutter
a ruff of feathers
and she follows the pattern
laid out for her.

But what she says is
not for him
for her merely
that later she shall say
he said and then I said
and then he said.

A. Passel

Revisions are hard work. There are the various areas to be worked on. The poet changes the wording to clarify sound, to sharpen images, to bring harmony and balance to the poem. Here is the final version.

194

VESPERS

(Final Version)

Partly turned aside, firm on the perch
she peers with circular bead-jet birdeyes
silent
subjected to the raucous harsh rough jeers
brooding--seeming to hear
by merely brooding.

And when he ceases
after one mad wild whirr of ineffectual fluster
filling her life with husk and dust
non-flying flight--
her turn:
she gives a flutter, a ruffling echo and
as predetermined
replies.

But what she cries
is non-assertive
responding merely in patterned dialogue
first he said and then I said and then he said.

A. Passel

Unit D. Assignment

Select one of your poems (preferably a new one
written for this exercise) and work out your revisions.
Make copies of each version of the poem and see if you
can notice a marked change between the first and last
version. Hand in all versions of this poem.

Module X

Evaluation as a Skill

Module X

Evaluation

This will be your final module. Here you will evaluate others and, finally, yourself.

There are various kinds of evaluation: you may judge writers as to their skill, their mechanical and technical proficiency. You may be interested in one special area of their writing: its unity, perhaps, or its poetic sound. You may judge the work aesthetically. You may read the work looking for reliable information or specific directions. Or you may be interested in the overall effect, the balance of all these qualities. But in all criticism covered by this course you will be safe in asking yourself these questions about the work you are evaluating:

Does the paper fulfill the requirements of the task the author attempted to accomplish? (Does it fulfill the assignment?)

Is it legible and mechanically sound?

Are the sentences clear and in the appropriate level of English? Right for the audience?

Do I know what the writer was trying to prove? Am I convinced? Was it worth saying? Remember that the writer has created his work to reach a specific audience. Always judge work in relation to this controlling factor.

Module X

Unit A

Judging Student Work

If you plan to teach, select one of the attached student themes best related to your level of interest: "My Ball Team" for elementary level, "Essay on Conrad" for high school level, "On the Beach" for college level.

ELEMENTARY LEVEL

(Notice that the events take place over a six-week period. You will want to talk to the student about the improvements made during this time. He must be a young boy: notice that he is still more interested in himself than in the group. Keep his age in mind when you criticize him.)

6/27

MY BALL TEAM

I play left field on my ball team.

In the first game we played this year we won.

We played a night game at 8:30. The score was 5-2. We had five. They had two.

We have won three games. We have lost three games. We are in third place. We may win the championship.

6/28

CHAPTER II

Now we are in second place because we won the game Tuesday night.

The score was sixteen to four. We really beat them.

In the game only one ball came to me. It was a fly and I caught it for the out. I was playing in left field.

At the plate I was up two times. One time I was out, but the other time I got a hit. It was a double.

CHAPTER III

We played on Friday, June 30. We won that game, too. The score was 8 to 7.

The last inning was the best. The score was tied at 7-7 when we came to bat in the bottom of the inning. Two guys got on base. Then the next batter hit a home run! It was really neat!

I was playing in left field this time. I didn't do too hot at the plate. I struck out twice and walked once. Next game I am going to do a lot better, I hope!

CHAPTER IV

This week our game was on Monday. The final score was 7-0. Guess what? They lost and we won! They are in first place but we beat them. It is the first game they have lost this season.

The last time we played them they won. Now we won. I wonder what would happen if we could play them again?

We have only three more games to play. I sure wish the season wasn't nearly over.

In the game I got a sacrifice when I hit the ball to the pitcher and the runner on second base made it to third base. But I was out.

CHAPTER V

Can you guess how our game came out last night? We won! The score was 11-2. We were the home team.

I never even got to bat. The first three innings I was in the dugout. Then I played the fourth inning. I was on deck when the last out was made. When we came up to bat in the bottom of the fifth inning I would have been the first batter. It was four minutes to eight and we had to quit at eight o'clock. So, the coach called the game and I never even got to bat once. But we won, anyway.

Our pitcher is so good they almost never even get a hit off him. He is a good batter, too. He got two good hits that bounced over the fence. The ground rules make those hits doubles. But sometimes he hits a real home run.

7/17

CHAPTER VI

On Friday night, July 14, we won again, 13-7.

There are seven teams and we play each team two times. That makes fourteen games for the season.

One inning the other team loaded the bases and the next batter hit a home run over the left field fence where I was playing. It was the first time someone hit a home run past the field I was playing.

Our very last game was on July 21. We won by a score of 7-0. I got on base once but got put out when I slid into third base trying to steal.

We are in second place in the league, but the first place team has 2 more games to play. So, if they get beat we may end up in a tie, or if they get beat both games we might even win the championship! It sure would be neat if we finally end up in first place!

HIGH SCHOOL LEVEL

(This student is a high-school senior: decide what skill you feel she had better concentrate on. Think of what you can have her do to overcome her most basic problem. The student was given this assignment: respond briefly to this quotation: "I wondered how far I should turn out faithful to that ideal conception of one's own personality every man sets up for himself secretly." From **The Secret Sharer** by Joseph Conrad.)

ESSAY ON CONRAD

Society: this is one of the most confusing and influential parts of everyone's life. Our society causes us to be and live just the way we are now.

Every person has his own set of ideals. Society helps form these ideals by different ways. Competition is very common. Although it may not show on the outside--people have a want to "Keep up" with someone else.

An environment has a very extreme effect on peoples' ideals. In a very rough neighborhood, competition would be greater. Besides this, coming from a very poor family makes one want to do better.

In reference to the quotation, every man should seek out their ideals. One needs an environment and competition to form his morals then carry them out to the fullest possible:

If no one carried out their ideals--we would not be in the fine shape we are. The inventions, medical milestones, and of course our freedom. The freedom our

204

forefathers wanted and did their most possible to achieve.

People cannot forget their ideals or leave them to someone else. It would cause everyone to come to a complete standstill. Our world would not be the same as it takes all kinds of people and ideals to make it.

COLLEGE LEVEL

(This student has submitted a short story designed to arouse poetic response in the reader. Note her stylistic device of repeated sentence pattern. How can you help her become an even better writer?)

ON THE BEACH

It was hot, a sticky, sweaty heat that the slight breeze blowing in from the ocean could do nothing to counter. It was gray, an overcast, faded, sun-lost day that occurs occasionally on the southern coast of California. Near the shore the ocean laid listlessly, almost motionless except for an infrequent swell that broke out against the rocks and lost its momentum before reaching the beach. The seagulls seemed to feel it was too dismal a day to fly, and instead waded in the shallows and the rock pools. The sands were only sparsely populated with people, scattered randomly from the rocks to the pier, from the sea wall to the water.

Spread close to the sea wall was a gray and purple patchwork quilt on which a woman lay like an ancient Aztec sacrifice to the sun, spreadeagled on her back. A bottle of Spanada was wrapped in wet towels and buried to its neck in the sand beside her with a straw protruding from its mouth. The woman's purblined eyes were shielded by smoky glasses from the sun. The quilt was stained with faded purple blotches. As the gray of the day intensified, as the sun caused purple heat waves to rise from the rocks and the sand, the woman was only seen to move when she sucked wine through the straw.

206

In the late afternoon a storm far out beyond Point
Concepcion formented a heavy wind which whipped away
the gray, for it cooled the air currents which blew on
the beach and sent big waves surging into shore. The
whole color of the formerly gray and depressing day
changed to stimulating blue, green, yellow. People
along the shore could see two skindivers that were in
trouble fighting the breakers that were threatening to
smash them against the rocks. As fear and excitement
spread, a Coast Guard helicopter flew in from the east
and dropped two men in wet suits into the water, then
released a pulley with which the divers were pulled
into the waiting helicopter.

The woman did not move even when the sun set and
the sky darkened, when the water grew black and the
sands grew cold. Fires were built on the beach, hot
dogs were burned and eaten, families played and went
home. Finally the beach was empty and she was alone,
except for the lights from a tanker coming in to
unload, and for the sea.

Unit A. Assignment

Evaluate one of these themes according to the questions listed in the introduction to this unit. You will have to imagine an appropriate assignment which has been given. Write an evaluation of this paper for the student. First comment on the strengths of the paper and then decide on the one area which you feel needs the most concentrated work on the part of the student. How can the writing be improved?

Alternative Assignment
Judging Clarity of a Report

If you are not going to teach, select a report in the area of your interest, a college student's work, a professional report in a professional journal, or a report delivered to a special group. Include a copy of this report with your assignment. Write an evaluation of the report as though the author had asked you for your criticism. Indicate, first, the strengths of the writing, then the areas which you feel could be improved in a future article. (Remember: this one is already in print.)

Module X

Unit B

Grading Student Work or Critical Approaches

Recently a panel of high school English teachers met together to talk about something that is very important to all of us and that is: how does a teacher evaluate a student? They began discussing questions important to all teachers and to those who are just facing the idea of becoming teachers.

TEACHERS' PANEL

Q: We turn to you because you are active intelligent teachers, experiened in an area which we are investigating: the problems of evaluation. May we begin with a basic question? If we assume that what you are really after is good work from your students, how do you decide what is "good work"?

Mr. F: I know good work, I think, when I read a paper and say to myself, "There is good work."

Mr. O: That's like looking at a painting or a sculpture and saying, if it pleases, it's good work. Actually in the final analysis, when we ask what is "good work," we must recognize that the companion question must be good work to whom? The student has his idea of what good work should be, the teacher has his, and colleges, parents and a variety of people concerned with that work have theirs. This then

209

necessitates criteria to be set, but these criteria are less than perfect instruments so at best we can only approximate a fair evaluation of good work.

Ms. C: I think that over a period of time you do develop some sort of an absolute that you grade against.

Ms. G: Yes, and when you know what reasonable standards are, you know when a piece of work is beyond that; when it shows some creativity or imagination or when the student has done something with the assignment that shows initiative.

Mr. O: But watch out. Don't be inflexible. You have to change your standards to fit the changing class. Each year we get a different crop of students and these students are sometimes better, sometimes worse. They never can really be called an average class. There's no such thing really as a class we should treat as an average class. New teachers have to recognize that.

Mr. F: I think that probably the most common link I find among new teachers in my department is that their expectations are unrealistically high. Their grades are lower because their standards are higher; they're fresh out of the academic milieu.

Ms. C: On the contrary, though, we have seen teachers come in new to our school and they tend to be terribly lenient with their students, giving much higher grades than they will in a couple of years.

Mr. O: We're still talking about averages. But teachers and classes individually aren't average.

Q.: I'm wondering about the far-from-average student. Suppose you have a student who comes into class and we'll say he's not very bright, he's not an "achiever." How do you judge what grade you're going to give him? Suppose that during the semester he doubles his output, raises his level to something fabulous for him, even though it's still nowhere near the rest of the class. Does he get an A?

Ms. C: I think any teacher is impressed by that kind of a change because, in the first place, it happens so rarely. But if the class were a college preparatory class, he would still have to come up to A work, regardless of the change. I might say, though, that the teacher who, out of concern for the C-D student's psyche, gives that student an A or B, is creating, in the long run, a far more shattering experience when, at the college level with more at stake, the student discovers he cannot compete academically.

Ms. G: Well, in my grading I try to give as much consideration as possible as to the student's ability and to what he has accomplished for that ability. But we find it difficult to give him college recommending grades on report cards. Now on certain specific assignments, if students have done an outstanding job, I reward them.

Mr. O: That goes along with my basic rule: treat each student as a special case as much as possible.

Q: Here's another question: in facing a class and working out how you're going to evaluate the class, do you find that you give equal time to the good student and the poor student?

Mr. O: I think it depends on the teacher. Once again you have teacher preferences. One might feel the good student is worth more so he will get more of his attention -- also he is a little bit more challenging to the teacher and many teachers like this. On the other hand, I suppose that there is something within all of us that wants to reach out and help the one who is not quite as capable.

Ms. C: What do you mean by giving more time? Do you mean help in academic work or just simply talking? Because some students seem to demand more.

Mr. F: Yes, but isn't that usually the academically capable student? I think mostly the bright kid is the one who stays after school, stays after class because he wants to finish a point that the bell interrupted; and the more passive, the more acquiescent student is more relieved that class is over.

Ms. G: But I find I have average and below-average students who demand as much or more of my time just in helping with academic work: "How do you do this assignment?" "Am I doing this right?" "How do I start this one?"

Ms. C: And I have a number of students who just come in with the rationalization that they want to talk

212

about their work, but they really just want to talk.

Mr. F: Talking is important. Socrates, when asked by his friends what they could do for his sons, replied, "Trouble their minds as I have troubled yours." This is basically the charge I would place on the new teacher.

Q: As a final question let's return to a further consideration of grades. The real question is, "Do grades matter?"

Mr. O: When we talk about a grading system, we are talking about a system that is set up on three levels: the students' level, the teacher's level, and the level of the system. But grades matter, I think, more to the students than to the teachers. It's a measuring device. We have to have some measuring device to decide the initial question, what is good work. But do the grades make a difference in the student's ability? I think the obvious answer is "no." He's not a better student because he got an A, he's a better student because he was capable of getting the A. Or, he may learn more getting a C than someone else who is getting an A. So in that sense, I don't think grades matter at all.

Mr. F: Obviously, grades make a difference! Our grading system depends enormously on what colleges and universities will accept. Our hands are tied and have been for a great many years. Colleges and universities say this is the standard we will look for as a standard for entrance. That grade is important.

Ms. C: Grades are terrifically important. Many kids are definitely thinking ahead to college and they're pushing very hard for grades -- they are so anxious about their grades.

Mr. O: If colleges would demand that students take an entrance exam, could we abolish the grading system for that purpose at least? And do you think it would make any difference?

Mr. F: I hate grades, partly because I hate to give them, but anyway I think they're terribly confining. We encourage a student to stay with the courses we know he can handle, classes where he feels safe because he thinks he can pass. I think the grade thing is terribly stultifying.

Ms. C: Do you ever talk to your students about that? I have. And our students say that they want the grades. They're being judged all through their lives and this is simply another form of it.

Unit B. Assignment

Review the ideas put forward by the members of this panel. Make note of the idea which seems of greatest interest to you. Write a presentation of this idea as you see it:

> Determine your audience
> Establish in your own mind what your bias is on this subject
> Argue as rationally as you can in favor of your belief
> Keep to one unified thesis

Alternative Assignment

If you prefer, seek out a specialist in your field of interest. Request an appointment for an interview. At that interview discuss with your specialist what is acknowledged to be the most valuable periodical or journal in the field which could help you understand the problems of your chosen area. Inquire about what help you can expect to receive from professional writing in your field. Write a report on this interview.

Module X

Unit C

Attitude Toward Peer Writing

Now you are ready to evaluate the writing of other students taking this course. Attached is a packet of sample exercises from various students. As you study the work, ask yourself these questions:

Did the student understand the wording of the assignment?

Does the answer deal with the question asked?

Is the answer based on some sort of organization?

Does the punctuation help the reader?

Are the words spelled correctly?

Are they used correctly?

Do the sentences have variety and interest?

Is there a beginning, a middle, and an end?

Is the overall effect what the student intended?

STUDENT PACKET: MODULE I

(Assignment: "In a brief essay identify the
audience. Explain how you made this identification.")

Excerpt number six seems as if it is taken from a
newspaper. The vocabulary is fairly simple and direct,
yet in a story form. Soap-box racing is not common in
California so it is my belief that the article is from
previous history or another part of the country. The
writer's choice of words seems fairly elementary as if
the audience could be children.

Many children of today, at least the ones I am
acquainted with, would not know about soap-box racing.
Therefore, the reader's previous knowledge would
influence the understanding. The writer, however, was
unaware of this. Perhaps it was written a number of
years ago.

The level of diction is not complicated, but rather
straight-forward. It seems like a newspaper article or
a children's text book so it can be said to be the
usual, standard diction that we expect in printed
matter. The only colloquialism would be that of the
subject -- the soap box racing. The rest of the
reading material could easily be that of ordinary and
popular usage for the day.

The meaning is effected in the way it is
structured. There are several simple sentences with
some quotes. The form is one that is familiar to text
book stories and that of a rather disjointed newspaper
article. The sentence structure is simple, with no
real repetitious patterns that can be followed.

217

The audience is limited because of the subject matter. A fellow racer or friends and relatives of the people mentioned in the passage would be most interested.

The writer is making an account of the race, the winner, and what it means for the future. He also is trying to convey the winner's attitude. The intentions of the author does not necessarily limit the audience.

(Assignment: "Select one TV viewing experience and analyze what is being done to you. Determine the bias of the program material. Identify the devices used to persuade you. What was the factual content of the program or segment? What audience was this material intended to reach? How was it slanted? How effective do you believe it was? How effective would it have been if it had been presented without bias?")

BIAS AND TRUTH

"The Devil's Triangle" was a television program filmed and produced by Richard Winer, and was designed to give the audience a feeling of the unknown.

The filming was done in and around an area known as "The Devil's Triangle," which is a large area in the Atlantic Ocean off the coast of Florida and which extends into the Caribbean. The area was never completely outlined, but it does come in as close as within one mile of Miami. Many strange and still unexplained things have happened in this area. Ships have disappeared; airplanes, both propelled and jet, have disappeared and nothing has ever been found of the ships, the planes, or the men.

One of the most effective devices used to persuade the audience was the narration of Vincent Price (the actor who is the Master of the horror movie). His voice actually could send chills down the spine as he described the many mysterious happenings in this area. Also, there were a number of interviews of people who "almost" were on a boat or plane that disappeared, of people who were involved in the knowledge of the loss and of the searching. Toward the end there were several people, among them an anthropologist, who discussed the theory of a magnetic field and/or flying saucers which might pick up these vessels. Though it may sound somewhat unrealistic, by the time the program was over, it was almost impossible not to believe that something supernatural had happened to these vessels.

(Assignment: "Something pleasant has just happened in your personal life: write about it in three short friendly letters (1) to an older member of your family, (2) to a close friend, and (3) to someone you respect out of your past associations. . . .")

FRIENDLY LETTERS

(a)

Dear Grandma,

Just a brief note to tell you of some great news. All your words of encouragement and support of my love for art makes this time more special to you and me. Remember the landscape I painted while visiting you last spring?   I entered it in the local art contest and it won a blue ribbon!   And that isn't all. . . . it has gone to a bigger festival and won second place there! Isn't that great?

I had to write you about it because you've always been so understanding and supportive of my interest in art from the time I was a little girl.   I will write more in a couple of days.

Much love,

Suzie

(b)

Dear Julie,

Hope this letter finds you and your new mate fine and enjoying marital bliss.   Are you still planning to come down next week-end for a visit?   We are looking forward to seeing you and showing you around.

I have a surprise to show you when you come.

221

Remember that art class we took together and how we used to tease about the day one of us would sell our work for thousands? Well, I haven't sold anything, but I have won an award for a landscape I did. So, while you're here, remind me to take you to see it if we have time.

Bring some dressy clothes and we'll go out for dinner to the new lodge I told you about. Can't wait to see both of you!

Love,
Susan

(c)

Dear Dr. Simms:

You might remember me as Susan Todd, a student in your art class at the college three years ago. I felt the need to write to you of some nice recognition I've received for a landscape I did this past year. You were a great influence in my life. Any skills I might have that enabled me to reach this point of achievement is due largely to your instruction and constant encouragement.

Therefore, it is important to me to let you know of my first place ribbon in a local show and second place honors in Theodore Van Tonnigan's Memorial Art Festival.

Thank you for your past supportive assistance and expert instruction.

Sincerely,
Susan (Todd) James

STUDENT PACKET: MODULE VII

(Assignment: "Write a story [or the major portion of a story] which reveals conflict.")

THE DRAGON

There had not been a dragon in our part of the realm for over a century. There had been several reports of sightings made up in the northern marshes, but few people paid any serious attention to them. The land was prospering and all who wished could travel the roads openly without fear.

I took to horse and set out upon my quest in the early part of March. Like the others before me, I had no specific idea as to which direction my way lay. I could do nothing but trust to chance and my own judgment. There had been strange rumors coming out of the east for months along with dark rumblings that hinted at another Great War. I resolved to travel eastward. With no other companions but my horse and squire, I set out upon the eastern road. It felt good to be out-of-doors again with the sun overhead and the wind in my face.

We had journeyed only three days when the weather began to change. Clouds drove the sun from the sky. There was thunder and lightning in the distance along with the promise of rain. We searched for some type of shelter but the land was barren and inhospitable. There was a storm brewing and the last thing I needed was a suit of rusty armor. We had just come to the top of a small hill and had stopped to rest when he came into view.

I had never seen anything like him. He was at least thirty feet long from snout to tail. He was not scaly, as one would imagine a dragon to be, but had a somewhat beaded appearance and was a brownish-red in color. A thin wisp of smoke issued forth from his nostrils and disappeared into the stormy sky. He saw me and eased his stride and cautiously approached until he was within speaking distance.

"Good morrow, sir knight," said he. "'Tis indeed a pleasant day for riding. Whither goest thou?"

"That is my own business and should not concern thee," said I.

"Oh, but it does concern me, for you are passing upon my highway and I shall demand a toll. Whether that toll shall be light or heavy depends on your ability to curb your saucy tongue."

"Why you insolent worm! That you should demand a toll is ridiculous and illegal. This is the king's road and all men travel freely upon it. What gives you the right to tax those who wish to use it?"

"It's very simple," he replied. "I was here first. I was here before thy precious, petty potentate was even thought of. Besides that, I can breathe fire and smoke. I can smash trees with my tail. I can crush cattle with my bare claws and I'm also bigger than you, so, there!"

He then drew himself up to his full height. He stood there towering before me and I must admit, he was rather large.

"How much do you want?"

He now began to stroke his chin with one of his front claws.

"'Tis been a cruel sore winter with me and I am in much need of nourishment. I feel that either thy horse or thy squire will serve quite well."

I was now in somewhat of a quandry. Which one should I give him? That squire had always been rather insolent while my horse had been unruly and hard to manage ever since I had acquired him. I finally decided upon my squire. The horse would probably have been the better choice but one of my position should never be seen on the open road afoot. I turned to my squire and found that, to my surprise, he was nothing more than a black speck disappearing into the west.

"It seems that you now have no choice," said he, "so, kindly dismount. I am beginning to get impatient and am quite tired of waiting."

"Nay, I shall not. It would not be seemly nor dignified if I were to be seen walking. I would not dare show my face at court again. They would laugh me straight out of the palace. Are you sure that there is nothing else I could do?"

"Positive."

"I was afraid of that."

I was hoping to avoid what promised to be rather violent and thoroughly distasteful confrontation. It now seemed inevitable. It's not that I don't like fighting dragons; it's just that I can think of a multitude of things that I would much rather do. This fellow was beginning to fume and become quite nasty.

"Are you going to dismount or am I going to be forced to devour both you and your horse?"

Well, I saw that there was going to be no getting around him, so I felt that I had, at least, better try and make a good showing of myself.

"Why, you over-grown, smoke-fuming salamander! Sup on me wouldst thou? Thou shalt get nought but cold steel for thy dinner and shall finish thy meal in hell should I have my way. Defend thyself!"

I shouldered my lance, lowered my visor, and spurred my mighty steed onward into the fray. He refused. Apparently my mighty steed was in no way ready nor willing to charge into the gaping, fire-breathing jaws of what was now a very infuriated dragon. The more I spurred him on, the more resolute he became. How does one go about extricating oneself honorably from such a situation. The huge beast was not going to give me any time to find out. With a blinding blast of flame, he charged. My horse, having more sense than his rider, immediately turned and ran. Unfortunately, to aid in his escape he had thrown off all excess baggage which included myself.

This was an embarrassing situation. There I lay, flat on my back with nothing between me and an enraged, charging dragon but my one lance. The beast was so intent upon his charge that he completely ignored the location of my lance's head. The next thing he knew was that he had been spitted like a roasting-chicken. He vaulted into the air vomiting smoke and fire then convulsed upon the ground then lay still. To my utter astonishment the huge beast began to disappear in a

mist.   He   dissolved   before   my   eyes.   Night   was
beginning   to   fall   so   I   found   some   small   shelter   and
tried   to   sleep.   I   had   killed   my   first   (and   only)
dragon.

That   morning   I   located   my   horse   and   returned   to   my
village.   I   needed   a   new   squire   and   also   needed   to
refresh   myself.   Slaying   a   dragon   can   be   a   hot   and
tiring   affair.   The   journey   back   was   uneventful   and   I
arrived   home   after   2-1/2   days'   ride.   I   immediately
went   to   the   local   inn   and   there   I   refreshed   myself   and
told   of   my   great   achievement.   Everyone   listened
breathlessly   and   when   I   had   finished   they   applauded
vigorously.   Everyone   in   the   room   wished   to   buy   me   my
ale   and   meat.   All   agreed   that   mine   was   the   best   tale
that   had   been   told   at   that   inn   in   many   a   year.   No   one
believed   me,   of   course.   Why   should   they?   There   hadn't
been   a   dragon   in   our   part   of   the   realm   for   over   a
century.

M. Carriker

(Assignment: "Look at something in nature. Let your imagination run free. Include an extended metaphor -- one metaphor carried throughout the poem.")

THE RAIN

The rain spatters against misted panes
And sounds like a dance of castanets.
A wet dog tucks his tail
And wanders aimlessly down the alley,
The water flowing along the gutter beside him.
Bleak and forlorn they wander away,
Dog, rain, and life.

P. Leigh-Pink

Unit C. Assignment

Evaluate each exercise, briefly and succinctly, and come to some conclusion concerning the student's writing skill. Write on the student's work (photocopy the pages or write in the book), showing where improvement is needed. Use moderation; remember, any student can only tackle one problem at a time. Always indicate misspellings, omitted or misused punctuation, faulty diction and grammar. However, center your attention on the most needed improvements. Include on a second sheet your final evaluation, as you would give it to the student. Be specific in your comments, let your suggestions be pertinent and your tone helpful.

Module X

Unit D

Self-evaluation

You have come to the last assignment in this course and it is time now for you to apply what you have learned to your own work. Look through your folder to gain a feeling of your style and competence. Test yourself against the guides given in this unit.

Unit D. Assignment

Write a self-evaluation, as objectively as you can. Always consider the audience you were trying to reach and the purpose of the communication.

Now you are ready for the final conference of the course. There is no final examination on course content. This conference will serve as the final evaluation of your work.

For the Instructor from the Author

For the Instructor from the Author

It will be perfectly obvious to you, no doubt, why I have selected the examples in this book. Some of the passages, like the one by Huxley in Module V, offer more material for discussion than we can squeeze into one session. Some material may seem less obviously usable. But each was chosen because I believe it offers students appropriate material to work with. I am sure you will be able to supplement this material with passages you know and like.

The most important material in this course is not in the book: it will be found in the exercises which the students submit to you. Particularly in this modularized approach to learning, we must recognize that each conference must include two areas of discussion: (1) the student's understanding of the ideas of communication presented in the module, and (2) the student's way of handling language as demonstrated by his answers.

I feel it is vital to use each conference as a learning session, not as a testing time. Marked progress can be made when instructor and student are able to discuss together the exact material which is needed by the student.

SETTING UP A SCHEDULE

This program has been taught successfully in our college for the last ten years. The material in the book has been repeatedly class-tested and adjusted for added strength. We find that students can handle one module every two weeks. For each of these two-week periods we schedule one half-hour individual conference for each student and one two-hour class meeting. During the class meetings we have a lecture-discussion-demonstration and time for a one-hour in-class theme. These themes give a clear picture of the student's progress throughout the course.

The surprise of unannounced topics for in-class themes gives the students a chance to rehearse that experience which we all know about: that demanding moment in life when we are suddenly required to produce a clear written statement with no preparation and no warning. It would be presumptuous of me, and counterproductive, if I were to suggest topics for these themes. I would like to offer you a list of suggestions for the in-class presentations, though, ones which have worked in this course in the past.

You will want to select a limited number of these or other topics to be presented in your bi-weekly meetings. Naturally, you may very well have your own ideas -- but in case you don't, here are some presentations you might try.

IN-CLASS PRESENTATIONS

Module I. Audience.
    I always meet my class as soon as possible when the term begins. Many students have never had this much responsibility for self-discipline. They need explanations and encouragement.

234

For demonstration: I ditto one passage from the local paper and analyze it to show what devices the author has used to reach his selected audience. Many students find difficulty in seeing beyond the subject matter of any passage. They must be shown how to get beyond the what into the how.

Module II. Being Organized.

For some students, this is the most revolutionary area they will study. Returning students particularly may have forgotten all they ever learned about note taking and outlining.

For demonstration: Have each student write one valid statement about a given subject (it can be as popular or as profound as you choose: on politics, aesthetics, ecology, domestic stress, campus flack). Collect the statements and read them aloud. Let the students decide what the thesis is going to be. Have them tell you how to sort the statements in three areas of persuasion. Use what you have collected to support the three-pronged argument. Let a student put this organized outline on the board. The class has outlined a paper.

Module III. Public Voice.

Here is a good chance to have a professional from the local radio or TV station come to your class to discuss the form and content of public service spots. If you can call on an instructor in media or audio-visual, usually such people are gracious about tempting students into their area.

If none of these is available to you, you might show a few live TV advertising spots in the class (you cannot go wrong here) and have the students, in groups of 4 or 5, prepare some statements about what they noticed about bias and persuasion.

Module IV. Letters.

A representative of the college placement service is often happy to talk to students about the subtleties of resumes and interviews. The large industries and businesses in your community (the ones which will probably hire a number of your graduates) usually offer to send interviewers from their personnel departments to discuss tactics and niceties.

If you have a leaning toward the dramatic, you may want to have a fictionalized encounter in which you interview a student, discussing the resume prepared in this module. Or perhaps another instructor can interview you. Such dramatizations can be both fun and effective.

Module V. Words, Words, Words.

Here is an opportunity for you to discuss major problems in student writing in general. I like to present "Ten Areas in Which Student Writing Can Be Strengthened." Many students have commented favorably on its effect on them.

1. The five common uses of the comma (in series, with parenthetic or introductory expressions, after the subordinate clause in an inverted sentence, before the conjunction in a compound

sentence, and with non-restrictive modifiers. Only this last usage requires much repeated explanation.) Students seem greatly relieved to find that there is some kind of limitation to comma usage. I manage to work in two uses of the semi-colon (in complex series and in compound sentences without conjunction). Actually, the students who learn these usages have got their punctuation pretty well in hand by the end of the lecture.

2. Syntactic balance in the construction of parallels and series. This is a discussion to help students avoid such disasters as "I like swimming and to ski."

3. Conceptual balance in the idea of parallels and series. We discuss comparable ideas and related items avoiding "You bring the salad, I'll bring the sandwiches, and it will probably rain."

4. Proper equation in sentences with linking verbs. This includes such disagreements as "The audience is adults."

5. Agreement of subject and verb. (And you know what I mean.)

6. Agreement of pronoun and referant. Some discussion must follow about "anyone, none, a person" and other pronouns, particularly when the antecedent is far removed.

237

7. Elimination of sentence fragments. This may involve a refresher course on the difference between verbs and verbals.

8. Reconstruction of run-on sentences, including comma splices and the never-ending monologue.

9. Judicious placement of modifiers and the avoidance of dangling constructions.

10. Three (possibly local) atrosities: _its_ vs _it's_, _alot_, and "Joe's Hamburger_'s_." Here you should add the misuses and malformations which particularly annoy you.

Module VI and VII. Fiction.

Students have respect for the work of other students, particularly if that work has appeared in print. Small discussion groups working on the two short stories in this module, "Will" and "Henery and Romand," will be able to point out the principles of short story writing. You might divide the problems among the groups, discussing any or all of these: revelation of human instincts, delineation of character, the creation of ambience, and selection and limitation in description (all discussed in Module VI). More advanced students might divide into groups to discuss: identifying conflict, hearing and reproducing natural dialogue, and dealing with various points of view (presented in Module VII). Reports from each of these groups to the whole class will probably stimulate even further open discussion.

Modules VIII and IX. Poetry.

If possible, invite three or four good student poets to come to your class for a presentation. I like to select poets who vary in age and persona, as well as those of each gender. Ask these poets each to read four or five poems which you have dittoed and distributed to the class. The poets will naturally explain, excuse, and augment the poems before and after they read -- this can hardly be avoided. But it is this kind of informality and human self-consciousness which particularly appeals to non-poetic students in the class.

Sometimes I have divided the class in quarters and have arranged for each poet to talk to each of the small groups in a kind of round-robin. Sometimes I have had the class submit questions which the poets know they will be required to answer. Often a panel discussion is most comfortable for student poets.

Here are a few questions we have asked with very satisfactory results:

What kind of person writes poetry?

What made you start writing?

Why do you write?

What conditions are most conducive to writing?

What is prose and what is poetry?

What are the elements a poem deals with?

Why do you use (or don't you use) rhyme?

239

Do you use traditional metered form?

Do you need a listener (reader)?

Do you need a critic?

Do critics harm you?

Who is your favorite poet?

Does that poet influence you?

Would you like to know that person?

What advice would you give a beginning poet?

Module X. Evaluation.

I almost always select this module for one of the discussion presentations. I have in the past invited bright and cooperative local high school teachers to come as a panel to discuss problems in evaluating student work. Now an excerpt from one such panel is included in the last module. Personally I feel so strongly about the force of positive and constructive evaluation that I usually give the presentation for this module myself. I want to impress on the students, whether they are going to be teachers or not, the dire need for a positive attitude in evaluation. Good parents, fast friends, congenial partners, and helpful associates all thrive on the atmosphere created by a positive attitude toward evaluation and criticism.

First, I feel that the students must learn that the evaluation should praise the best thing about the work being criticized. At times such a principle forces me to compliment the student on the wide margins, the clear handwriting, or the title of the theme. But at

240

any rate, we have started off with the idea that the student's total annihilation is not my immediate aim. Then an evaluator should be ready to tackle the lowest level of accomplishment and clear up the worse area first.

Every student should approach the material directly, looking for:
Appropriateness of material to assignment
Level of interest to the reader
Mechanical and structural proficiency
Particularly good words, sentences, or sections
Areas in which style could be improved
Indications of clear thinking or faulty logic
Best elements and those which could be improved

No matter whom they are criticizing, let's get them to discuss the most basic level first. After all, no writer can improve in all areas simultaneously. If all the basics are handled properly, a critic can begin to deal with the content of the composition.

Students find self-evaluation very difficult; that seems only natural. In this class meeting I feel that by making clear my criteria and approach for judging them, I am helping students to evaluate themselves. They need to develop an objectivity in reviewing their own writing, an objectivity which will stand them in good stead all of their lives. If in rereading their own work they do not gain such a perspective, the students may read the work aloud. We can hear weakness in our own work which would never come to our attention through our eyes alone. Even more effective is listening to our own words being read aloud by someone else. This generous and friendly reader may not be readily available. But this electronic age offers a system even more revealing. Writers who hear their own voices on tape, reading their own words, take part in a self-criticism not possible any other way. The ordeal is discomforting. The resultant self-criticism should make the whole experience worth the pain.

Such a procedure may be used in an abbreviated form in the classroom during this last class-meeting. Again try working in small groups (a practice which induces the reticent student to become vocal). Let each group work with a tape recorder, all students reading selections from what they consider their best work of the quarter. Peers in the group can then react to what the students say when they hear their own voice on tape.

STUDENT REPONSE

All in all, these modules work well when the students are willing to be concerned about their outside preparation and are willing to meet their commitments and keep their appointments. Students who cannot assume this responsibility should be urged to study composition in a more traditional course.

Those who can handle themselves in a modularized course really learn under this system. Good students are able to polish their style and overcome their boredom, thanks to individual conferences. Students with ingrained substandard usage and careless habits can concentrate -- under guidance -- on these particular areas without feeling that they are holding back the class. Creative students can practice form and usage while being encouraged to express their basic feelings. True, a rapid succession of individual conferences can tire the instructor. But I know of no system of teaching that offers a more satisfying way to take part in a student's progress.